The New Aradia

Also by Laura Tempest Zakroff:

The Witch's Cauldron:
The Craft, Lore and Magick of Ritual Vessels
(Llewellyn, 2017)

Sigil Witchery:
A Witch's Guide to Crafting Magick Symbols
(Llewellyn, 2018)

Weave the Liminal:
Living Modern Traditional Witchcraft
(Llewellyn, 2019)

Co-authored with Jason Mankey:

The Witch's Altar:
The Craft, Lore and Magick of Sacred Space
(Llewellyn, 2018)

The New Aradia
A Witch's Handbook to Magical Resistance

Edited by
Laura Tempest Zakroff

Revelore Press
Seattle
2018

The New Aradia:
A Witch's Handbook to Magical Resistance

Book and cover design by Jenn Zahrt.
Cover image and interior figures by Laura Tempest Zakroff.

ISBN 978-1-947544-16-1
Printed globally on demand through IngramSpark

First printed by REVELORE PRESS in 2018

REVELORE PRESS
220 2ND AVE S #91
Seattle, WA 98104
USA

www.revelore.press

The Charge of the New Aradia

When sense and world have parted ways,
Whenever need is great and dire
In brightest sun or moon's dark phase
Bring forth will to light the fire.
Send down the roots, raise up your arms,
Call forth spirit, summon its charms
With wand and cauldron, stang and knife,
With cloak and horn and lore of wife
Build your wisdom and bide your time
In eyes of heart, and blood sweet wine.
In city and wood gather still
To protect and guide with our will.
Now is the time to heed the call
Witches together one and all.
In our truth, we know the power,
That our voice brings down the tower.
To banish, cleanse, bless, heal, and guide
With our secrets and sabbat ride.
It's the hour to change the tides
For now as witches we all rise!

Laura Tempest Zakroff
1/25/2017
#WeAreAradia

Contents

The Charge of the New Aradia ~ 5
Laura Tempest Zakroff

A Call to Aradia ~ 11
Aidan Wachter

Introduction ~ 14
Laura Tempest Zakroff

The Power of Shared Magic ~ 18
Laura Tempest Zakroff

Aradia in the New Millennium ~ 20
Storm Faerywolf

We Are Aradia ~ 25
H. Byron Ballard

The Spirit of Rebellion ~ 27
Mat Auryn

Aradia—An Invocation ~ 31
Phoenix LeFae

Witchcraft Medicine for the Soul of the Land and People ~ 33
Christopher Penczak

Nine Garden Allies: Plants for Talismans, Spells & Actions ~ 40
Raye Schwarz

Diana's Protection ~ 44
Mat Auryn

Peace Oil ~ 47
Jenn Zahrt

Dragonroot: A Charm for (In)Visibility ~ 48
Casandra Johns

A Prayer to Aradia, in the Wake of Charlottesville ~ 51
Misha Magdalene

A Spell to Win a Court Case When Unjustly Detained ~ 54
Aradia the Rose

A Witch Bottle for Protection of Home, Family & Community ~ 59
Kelden

Baityloi: An Ancient Greek Method of Purifying Civic Institutions & Protecting Their Integrity ~ 61
Gwendolyn Reece

Aradia and the Armor of Flames ~ 66
Devin Hunter

Calming the Inner Storm Spell ~ 68
Ivo Dominguez Jr.

Two Spells for Water ~ 71
Annwyn Avalon

Water Devotional & an Oath to Protect the Water ~ 72
Lisa Bland

Creating a Sun ~ 74
Annalun

Prayer to the Great Mother ~ 75
Jay Logan

Blood Moon Eclipse Ritual ~ 77
Irina Xara

Resistance & Resilience / Resilience & Resistance ~ 81
Irisanya Moon

A Spell to Reclaim Your Sovereignty ~ 84
Deborah Castellano

House Cleansing Wash ~ 87
Lyssa Heartsong

A Spell for Good Housekeeping ~ 89
Stephen Pocock

A Ritual for Remembering Our Power & ~ 90
Remembering What We Are
Amanda Bell

An Invocation for Freedom ~ 93
Patti Wigington

ACKNOWLEDGEMENTS ~ 96
CONTRIBUTORS ~ 97
RESOURCES ~ 104

List of Sigils

The Power Sigil ~ 18

A Sigil to Protect Protesters & Those Detained by ICE ~ 57

A Sigil to Prevent Burnout, or the Anti-Burnout Sigil ~ 58

A Sigil for the Housing Crisis ~ 65

A Border Sigil, or a Sigil to Resolve Border Issues & Facilitate Healing ~ 83

A Sigil to Build & Strengthen Community ~ 92

A Call to Aradia

Aidan Wachter

IO Aradia!
Daughter of Lucifer
Cat-born
Firefly
Child of the Light

IO Aradia!
Daughter of Diana
Cat-born
Firefly
Child of the Night

Bring you the poison
Beautiful Sister
salt on the table
for tyrants and kings

Bring you the harvest
Beautiful Mother
a spell of great bounty
the downfall of lords

Bring me my lover
Witch Queen, Witch Mother
dog-ridden and wanting
close by my side

Bless thee my tongue
with the language of spirits
so I may command them
to find what I seek

Bless thee my ears
with the language of nature
that I may know
the words of the wind

My hands are your hands
Blessed Enchantress
the works that they do
are your work alone

My voice is your voice
Blessed Enchantress
the words that you speak
are the will of the world

IO Aradia!
Daughter of Lucifer
Cat-born
Firefly
Child of the Light

IO Aradia!
Daughter of Diana
Cat-born
Firefly
Child of the Night

Aradia!
Diana!
Rorasa!

Aradia!
Diana!
Rorasa!

Aradia!
Diana!
Rorasa!

Composed September, 2018

Note: This is a very simple general call/invocation to/of Aradia. It follows a standard pattern of identification leading to invocation. The spells or other work done after are to be considered done by Aradia herself, with the operant present as the vehicle through which the physical actions are performed. The final lines: Aradia! Diana! Rorasa! Can be repeated at length as mantra, trance induction, or invocation.

Introduction

These are the times we were made for.

THIS PHRASE CAME TO ME repeatedly through multiple trance workings nearly twenty years ago, but I did not fully understand the depth of its meaning in my younger days.

Back then, the words seem to apply to the blossoming of renewed interest in Witchcraft and the issues involved with navigating that path in a world that did not want to accept or understand Witches. We had to fight to be properly represented in the media, to celebrate our ways without harassment, to have representation in court and on councils, to have our symbols etched on our gravestones. So much has changed in terms of legal recognition as well as cultural familiarity over the years, thanks to the work of many people taking risks to push against stereotypes, provide education, and challenge the system. It is not perfect or universal, but things have come a long way in a relatively short amount of time.

Yet...those words also were accompanied by visions of great change and turmoil, followed by a new sense of order and renewal, like a sunny clear sky after a violent storm. I pondered if the chaos referred to something personal in my own life or something larger in the world. When my life totally imploded and then reformed into something amazing, I felt content to assign the meaning of the vision to that pattern. Mostly comfortable, but not entirely because it still lurked just out of sight, like a worrisome loose thread you keep tucking back into a sweater.

Then throughout 2016, various parts of the world got a rude wake-up call that things were really not what they seemed. There was—*and still is*—much work to be done. Real change must happen from government, legislation and social responsibilities, to how we live on and with this planet and each other. But it can be very challenging to decide just how to manifest that change.

You can try to cause change from the top, like trimming a towering tree or cutting back a bramble thicket. That will alter how things look—for a little while at least. But the system is still left intact, and like the mythical hydra, it can and will sprout another head, eventually.

To effect real change, you must start at the root level. There are many ways to do this. You can try to pull the whole thing out, roots and all. You can work the very soil it grows in by changing the quality and chemistry of the earth. You could introduce a competitive species that might push out the offending plant, fighting it for resources. If one is trying to protect surrounding plants that are suffering under the shade of the problematic growth, you could triage the damage and try to give those fragile ones more support. Another way is by investing time and effort into growing things that are better suited for the soil and provide greater benefit to the community. There is no one way, and you can very easily get caught up in arguing just who is right—and inadvertently never changing anything at all.

So what does this all have to do with Witches and Witchcraft?

At the heart of Witchcraft is change. We work magic in the microcosm to affect the macrocosm—whether that is personal change within us, in our immediate environments, or the larger world around us. Witchcraft happens through thoughts and words, actions and elements—mundane and metaphysical alike.

In 1899, the folklorist Charles Godfrey Leland published *Aradia or the Gospel of the Witches*—a collection of myth, poetry, and magical instructions. It centers around the story that the Goddess Diana saw that her people were suffering from tyranny and other abuses. So she sent her daughter Aradia to earth to teach them the secrets of Witchcraft so the people could defend themselves and rise up. Included within the Gospel are spells, rituals, and other tidbits that have supposedly been passed down for generations.

There are various theories and concerns about the source material for the Gospel, but no one can dismiss the fact that Leland's book has definitely played a role in the development of modern Witchcraft traditions. Getting caught up in arguing about authenticity and source material is a distraction. Instead, we need to look at the heart of the myth and consider what *Aradia* means for us today.

Wrapped within the pages of *Aradia* is the truth that Witchcraft is a revolutionary practice—a means for fighting against social injustices, shifting the balance of power, freeing people from oppression, breaking down political and financial systems that work against the people and nature itself. Witchcraft has long been the tool of the disenfranchised and the marginal. Calling oneself a Witch is in itself an act of defiance, a statement of going against the grain and the status quo of society. Most importantly: Witches get the work done.

We all are the modern-day Aradia. We do not need a savior, or one voice to save us—we are capable of saving ourselves and each other. It is time to step into our roles as teachers, protectors, guides, and leaders. We are being called upon to stand up, to build and use our practices to protect and to empower everyone who needs it: across traditions, genders, colors, creeds, ages, and abilities. We can revel in and honor diversity *and* bring everyone up together.

The New Aradia is a handbook for modern Witches, designed to serve as a collection of ideas to teach, fortify, balance, protect, illuminate, and guide. Within these pages you will find sigils, spells, recipes, essays, invocations, rituals, and more—all gathered from experienced magical practitioners. At your very fingertips is an arsenal of tools to aid you on your path. I hope that you will find this collection inspiring and empowering.

It is vital to note that every person can practice magical activism and resistance in their own way, to the best of their ability. Magical resistance happens both through physical means and metaphysical works—mind, body, and spirit. We should not forget to use the mundane methods available to us. Exercise your right to vote, encourage others to do the same, take part in your local government, stand up for others in your community, take care of yourself and those around you—these are all part of our path and practice. We seek not only to survive, but to thrive and craft new possibilities for tomorrow—for humanity, for the planet, for all.

Lastly, in tumultuous times as these, there will be much fear, doubt, anxiety, and worry. We will wonder if we have the strength or power to make it through. As Witches, we must face the storm and not give in to fear or despair. Remember: *These are the times we were made for.*

May the light of Aradia guide your way.

Laura Tempest Zakroff
Seattle, WA
September 2018

The Power of Shared Magic

Laura Tempest Zakroff

THERE ARE WORKINGS THAT BY DESIGN and nature should be secret, allocated to the realm of silence and unspoken mystery. Their power vibrates within the folds of dark velvet, felt yet unseen. They shift and cause change like roots below the earth, moving a little at a time: slow and steady.

By that same measure there are workings that are designed to be public, known, shown, and spoken. With every view or sharing, their power builds like a rising tide, making waves that cause change. They inspire, enthuse, and invigorate through their use and presence. They become an ocean that cannot be countered without great difficulty, because the waves can become endless, carving out the new landscape. Both kinds of workings are necessary, and it's crucial to know the right time and place for each.

Sigils are symbols (drawn, carved, painted, sewn, etc.) believed to have magical properties. The visual image, the method of physical application or metaphysical interaction, and most importantly the thoughts upon which the symbol is created—help unlock and empower the sigil. They continue to work subliminally behind the scenes—much like the operating system of a computer. They help us consider what we treasure, how we can manifest change in our personal worlds, and in turn affect the macrocosm. Little shifts of position, new inspirations, cracks of light filtering through: nothing too dramatic on the personal level, but still change that you can stand back and see as the mosaic comes together.

The sigils found within this book, by the heart of their design, function through both personal and shared magic. They affect change in both the micro and macrocosms. These sigils thrive by repetition, each use acting like a swelling wave of change. Others may seek to fight the wave, but the ocean cannot be stopped.

The Power Sigil

Laura Tempest Zakroff

Built into this sigil:

¶ protection of mind, body, and spirit

¶ recognition of the Other

¶ foster hope

¶ preserve personal power

¶ facilitate positive and effective change

¶ build new traditions of respect for all humanity

What to do with this sigil: This sigil is a mark to remind you of your own power, and to take action. It can be used anywhere: in your home, at work, on your body. You can print it out to look at, draw it again and again for yourself, make into a talisman, tattoo it on your body, trace it during meditation—whatever helps you connect with it and feel empowered.

Aradia in the New Millennium

Storm Faerywolf

ARADIA, according to folklorist Charles Godfrey Leland in his 1899 book of the same name, is a goddess of witchcraft, an avatar for the primordial goddess, Diana. She is the daughter of both Diana and Lucifer, the god of light, and hence she is described as having within herself the qualities and potentialities of both of her divine parents. She thus represents the "crooked path" of witchcraft; a path that offers bane as well as blessing.

The tale reveals her to be the first witch, sent to earth by her mother, Diana—Queen of the Witches and Faeries—to teach the poor and the oppressed the hidden arts of witchcraft in order to free themselves from slavery and even to torment their oppressors. While many of the poetic elements of Aradia would find themselves inspiring the creation of Gardner's Wicca (one needs only look to the "Charge of the Goddess," beautifully rendered by the late Doreen Valiente, as an example of this) the elements of *Aradia* that show the witch in a negative or threatening light have been largely ignored by the modern movement. This whitewashing gives us a publicly presentable version of the Craft, palatable to a "polite society," but in so doing thumbs its nose at an important cultural and folkloric stream of power that helped to create the modern movement. This, as well as ignoring the plight of many people in the here and now who likewise are suffering at the hands of an oppressor class, and who might benefit from an authentic and unneutered Craft.

While some would insist that the answer to oppression lies solely in non-confrontational actions (a laudable conviction, to be certain) this ignores the actual histories of oppressed peoples and their struggles toward liberation, recasting their efforts into either that of criminality, or reduced to vaguely affirming platitudes that end up serving the status quo by helping to prevent any substantive change from taking place. Philosophies that chastise the disempowered for using tactics that are unpleasant are an instrumental part of the system which seeks to suppress *all* displays of opposition, not just those that are violent or dangerous. For a clear example, we need look no further than the conversation surrounding the National Football League in the US and the peaceful protest of players like Colin Kaepernick, who chose to #TakeAKnee during the national anthem in order to highlight the severe problem of police violence toward black communities. Taking the knee during the anthem was a peaceful way to draw attention to the fact that "the land of the free and home of the brave" has effectively only been a reality for a certain class, namely white people. These protests were recast in the public eye as protesting the anthem itself and the freedom that this country is said to represent. The irony of this is certainly lost on those who would seek to even criminalize such actions, but in a capitalist society the most effective weapons are economic. At the time of this writing, Mr. Kaepernick still has not been signed onto a team despite his obvious talent and is currently involved in a court battle against the NFL for being politically blacklisted.

For witches, Aradia is a reminder that our Craft serves first and foremost the underclass; that our very heritage is one of liberation and equality; and also that sometimes in order to survive, we must also fight back.

While not all witches will be called to use their magic in a martial manner, our history shows us that—at the very least—this type of work is part of our heritage and cannot be simply ignored. All too often witches will condemn those who engage in such practices and judge them as not being "real" practitioners of the Craft, as if we ever claimed to be in possession of a singular moral code. While certain branches of the Craft may have legitimate prohibitions against such types of workings, such as some interpretations of the Wiccan Rede ("An it harm none, do what ye will") this is so very far away from any sort of consensus universal to us all. The Faery tradition, for example, has no such moral restrictions on cursing work—a quality we share with many other forms of what has come to be called, "traditional witchcraft". Regardless of one's personal convictions, we can easily and factually state that cursing and hexing is part of the witches' repertoire, and those who engage in it should not be excluded from the banner of witchcraft.

The mythology put forward in *Aradia* is one of opposition to oppression, and specifically the ruling class. Aradia is sent to teach witchcraft and the art of poisoning so that the masters "may die in their palaces." Not exactly the happy-go-lucky version of the Craft postulated in the latter years of the twentieth century. Those who would insist on others minding the "Threefold Law" might be interested to know that *Aradia* poses a sort of *two*fold law, when it is affirmed:

> And when a priest shall do you injury
> By his benedictions, ye shall do to him
> Double the harm, and do it in the name
> Of me, Diana, Queen of witches all!

For those of us who are called to this type of work, *Aradia* is also a reminder of the divine responsibility that comes with it. She was not sent to teach the art of the witches' craft to the merely annoyed or even to the righteously angry... she was sent to teach the *poor* and the *oppressed*. In this we begin to see an emerging ethical stance, even if it has gone largely unnoticed by a privileged class which denies basic human dignity to those it continually subjugates. The witch can be a force of justice that presents itself to those who have no other place to turn. To a desperate people, who are in danger of starving, of dying... who cannot feed their families or themselves... those who have been cast out... cast down into the streets and the gutters... to these people Aradia stands as a shining beacon of hope. And of personal power. For it is not Aradia who is coming to right our wrongs. She is our teacher, but she does not act for us. Whatever actions are taken, we will have to do them ourselves.

This is the thinking behind #WeAreAradia. We are not asking for some outside force to come in and fix our mess. We recognize that we need to fix it ourselves, and Aradia as a symbol reminds us to stay true to our ideals… to learn all the magic we can, and to put that magic to use, even when it is difficult or "harsh." Real witchcraft has teeth.

As a "spirit guide" Aradia can be instrumental for witches to help us learn deeper magics than what might be imparted by a human teacher, regardless of initiatory lineage. The most effective witches are not necessarily members of an old tradition or even of a functioning coven! The most powerful witches might of course be those things, but what sets a witch apart is their knowledge and their power, and this is accumulated by the hard work of showing up and communing with the spirits of nature, painstakingly learning what secrets they may have to offer, and then putting them into practice. If you have not yet begun working with the spirit of Aradia, I encourage you to do so. Using whatever tools your individual traditions may offer, reach out to she who is the first of the witches, the original teacher of the Craft. May her spirit guide us as we resist in our own ways.

A Modern Invocation to Aradia

Diana, the primordial womb of all
Divided into dark and light
And kept the darkness for herself
While Lucifer did shine so bright.

She pursued him, he did flee
She did infringe his sovereignty.
And from their union, *she* was born:
Behold: the Darkly Radiant One.

The New Aradia

Hail, Aradia!
First of all the witches known!
Who came to teach the witching arts,
To all the fallen and the low.

Hail, Aradia!
Born of darkness and of light
We call your power into us;
That we may embody here your righteous might.

May your darkness and your flame
Guide our actions, in your name
And may those actions shatter every chain!
Bringing justice and easing pain.

Daughter of witchcraft who inspires,
Who stokes the solemn, ancient fires
That burn for freedom and the deep desire
To know all that can and does transpire
Behind nature's opaque curtain
To see beyond that which was once thought certain,
To learn of the forbidden mysteries,
Not contained in official histories;
The most powerful of all the witcheries:
The liberation of the soul.

IO, Aradia!

We Are Aradia

H. Byron Ballard

It is two nights until the moon is new—a sharp hook slashing through the black sky, ominous in its brightness. There is a job of work set aside for these Nights Before, these dark moon nights. There are allies here: the Dead, the land spirits, plants that cure and plants that kill. Witches who know the work, who do the work.

Wort and bane. Tooth and bone. Hair and iron.

For so long now—longer than I care to remember, truth be told—I have been teaching about and pondering this roiling Tower Time that we have come to inhabit. These times require a kind of insanity in those who address them. We cast about, wild-eyed, clinging to our companions, reaching blindly for tools. And for agency. And for something like hope.

Platitudes are not helpful but a well-placed meme brings a snort of laughter, a gleam of solidarity. The work. If we only knew what to do, we could do it. We could, but would we? As empire again collapses upon itself—this Mt St Helens of broken culture—we crouch like hares before the Mower, hesitating to run when faced with a shrieking loudness that also blinds us, leaving us immobile, powerless.

Put that aside now. Set your face against the gathering cold, the meanness of spirit that threatens to wither us before our time. Dig your heels into the good old Earth. Remember who you are. Consider your deepest birthright as witches. Gather your allies. Sharpen your tools.

We were never domesticated here in the hill country, never were tame witches, coming when called. You aren't either. You got smarts and guts and all the necessaries. We are going to need that—and each other—as we face this world we have built, these revenants of culture that comfort and repel us.

We stand at dark moon and the tools for our work are laid out in readiness.

Witches, time to ride.

The Spirit of Rebellion

Mat Auryn

WITCHCRAFT SEEMS TO BE something that emerges organically within every spiritual and religious culture. It is not something you can ever destroy, hard as some may try. History has shown the attempts by any group to do so are never entirely successful. Attempts at "killing off the witches" can never thoroughly destroy the spirit of Witchcraft itself. Witchcraft is like a weed with strong roots. Here I feel the weed is the perfect illustration, a sturdy plant often with overlooked medicinal or poisonous properties, which is rejected as unwanted. Cutting off the surface part of the plant will never be successful and will only make it regrow stronger.

Witchcraft does not emerge from a vacuum. If you look at history and you look at the use of the word "witch" within these cultures you will see that Witchcraft appears as a balance to the predominant culture. Witchcraft is about power and maintaining a balance with that power. I believe that magic arises naturally within any culture and can be utilized and embraced by anyone or any religious tradition—but Witchcraft is another creature, it is the magic of otherness.

Even within Pagan societies, including those who embraced magic, there were still the witches—the outcasts, the heretics, those who would do what the priests wouldn't. For example, the Greeks were a polytheistic society that embraced the magic of theurgy—yet there are still writings about the witches who performed rites and rituals that defied the cultural attitudes of the overarching religion. I believe that this explains the emergence of witchcraft traditions such as Satanism, in response to the growing power of the Christian Church. It also describes the development of Witchcraft traditions that are Earth-Centered practices in a world where we begin ignoring and destroying the Earth as a purely meaningless creation of a distant Creator.

I believe the Bible is spot on when it says "For rebellion is the sin of witchcraft, and stubbornness is as iniquity and idolatry..." in 1 Samuel 15:23. This is why the story of Aradia is so compelling as a myth—be it entirely fictional or reminiscent of older hidden legends. In the tale, Diana sends down Aradia to empower the oppressed with the power of Witchcraft. This myth is a central myth to my tradition of Witchcraft, Sacred Fires. In short, Witchcraft is the gift of power to the marginalized. Any culture you decide to look at in history, you will see a theme of Witchcraft emerging as a response to the lack of power. It arises as a tool for justice, a tool to maintain balance and to level the playing field through rebellious spiritual practices.

In *The Witch's Book of Power*, Devin Hunter refers to Diana as the Goddess of the Island of Misfit Toys. And this is a compelling piece of insight if you meditate on it. Diana, as the Goddess of Witchcraft, empowers those whom society has rejected, who feel powerless, broken and lost. I believe that it is this formula that creates the right circumstances for the roots of Witchcraft to begin regenerating.

The power of Witchcraft is the power of otherness, and therefore, I do not believe it can ever honestly be a large organized religion—though it may be the tools of what resembles a religion, because Witchcraft is a universal response to religion's imbalance. It emerges to system-bust the institutions of dogma that begin threatening life, free will, and personal sovereignty. As such, it is only natural to see the new generation of Witchcraft evolving and reemerging as more feminist, queerer, browner, and more gender-fluid—because it is these folk who are being made to believe by those in political and spiritual power that they are misfit toys. It is the marginalized, and those who sympathize with them, who will bear the mantle of the Spirit of Witchcraft until they are no longer marginalized or oppressed.

Make no mistake; witchcraft is political. It has been political since the first kings summoned sorcerers for a strategic edge in war—to bind opponents, to gain political power, to give prophecy, or poison other kings. Witchcraft has been political since the first witches had to go into hiding and shroud everything in secrecy out of fear of persecution. Witchcraft has been political since the first person was tortured and killed under the accusation of witchcraft. Witchcraft has been political since the first witch performed abortions to desperate women leading to tales of killing or eating babies.

Witchcraft has been political since the first monotheists' armies came to destroy and desecrate Pagan sites and temples. Witchcraft has been political as long as witches have deemed the female body as equally divine and sovereign as the male body. Witchcraft has been political for as long as witches have made alliances, oaths, and pacts with Nature and Nature spirits, vowing to protect and honor. Witchcraft has been political ever since a witch decided to hold strong beliefs about what is right and what is wrong, regardless of what the institutions in power say. Witchcraft has been political as a group of marginalized folks outcast by society since the beginning.

The history of Witchcraft reminds us of what happens when people start singling out specific groups and classes of people and dehumanizing them. It reminds us of what happens when people start turning a blind eye, make excuses for, or even worse supporting the abuses of marginalized groups and classes of people. It reminds us of what happens when religion and state become a single force. It reminds us of how dangerous it is for those in political power to start whipping the public into a frenzy and to encourage violence against others.

We do not even have to look that far back to see what happens; we can merely look at World War II to find out. Knowing history is the ability to recognize that a fascist nationalist is committing genocide and drawing a parallel with that happening previously. Understanding history is the ability to identify the parallels every step along the way to a fascist nationalist committing genocide and then preventing it before it happens.

Aradia is the spirit of that rebellion, in communion with Her, she delivered these words. May they empower and inspire you as much as they did for me:

> Diana of the moonlight would not be owned by any man or god. She would strike down with swiftness those who attempted to hunt the Huntress and force her hand. Lucifer being of formless fire would not submit to Adam of clay and rebelled against God, refusing to sacrifice his dignity, pride, and power.
>
> From them, I was fashioned, moonlight and fire, darkness and light, so that witches would be truly free. Free to never be owned nor submit to any mortal or god. To rebel. To never sacrifice their dignity, pride, or power. Striking down all those who attempt to oppress the children of the Huntress and the Hunter. Shattering them one by one like clay pigeons, in Their Names.

Aradia—An Invocation

Phoenix LeFae

As a goddess, Aradia is much misunderstood. Many do not believe she is (or even was) a goddess. Her origins are full of plot holes and question marks, and honestly, this does not matter all that much anymore. There may be no proof that Aradia existed anywhere but in Charles Leland's imagination prior to 1899. However, since 1899 Aradia has taken on a life of her own. All over the world occultists, witches, wiccans, and ritualists call on her. Folks who took Leland's work as truth ran with the power of this goddess and built upon it. Now, she is gaining in popularity and recognition. Why might that be?

In Leland's myth Aradia was sent to earth to teach the common folk witchcraft. Through her the oppressed were shown how they could take their power back. She was sent to the human realm at a time of great need; to show a way to make real change; to reconnect people with their power.

At a time when people were hopeless, helpless, and struggling, they needed the power of witchcraft to turn the tides and bring hope. Hope is a powerful tool. And sadly, we find ourselves in a similar political and social climate. People are struggling again. The divide between people is getting increasingly larger, and we need something to bridge this gap, to bring us together. We need something, *someone* to remind us that we have the power.

The more that we call on Aradia, the stronger she gets—for what you feed with words and deeds grows. We cannot know the details of her origins, yet we can see what she has become and what she is becoming: a Goddess of witchcraft, power, and resistance.

The following invocation is a calling for Aradia's power. Use this invocation in rituals for Aradia, when you need a boost for your own personal power, or as a prayer for shifting the tides of oppression.

Invocation to Aradia

Aradia, Aradia, Aradia
Daughter of the heavens above
And the earth below
I call you

Bringer of witchcraft
Singer of power
Sower of magic
I call you

Guide me in the release of oppressive bondage
Bondage of others and of my own

Show me the way back to myself
My witchcraft, my power, my divinity

Connect me with my inherent gifts
Gifts of change, tenacity, and intuition

Aradia, Aradia, Aradia
First witch, resister, poisoner
Magician, priestex, healer
I call you

May you walk with me in power
May you fight with me for freedom
May you hold me in compassion

Blessed Be!

Witchcraft Medicine for the Soul of the Land and People

Christopher Penczak

WHILE I LOVE *THE GOSPEL OF THE WITCHES*, at heart I am not a Witch "red in tooth and claw" in my practices. I am not the wild man. I am more green in leaf and branch. My rebellion comes in simply living life outside of traditional norms. My revolution comes from creating teachings, groups, and community, and providing support and options for new ways. My resistance is in experimenting and building what might come next as older structures are dismantled. What will we do when the rebellion is over and we have won?

While I understand the proposed historic context of the Aradia passage, "And when a priest shall do you injury, By his benedictions, ye shall do to him, Double the harm, and do it in the name, Of me, Diana, Queen of witches all!" I find myself looking not just for resistance, but restoration. What is the form of restorative, not punitive, justice? Why did the priest end up being the priest, doing injury? Is the priest a victim of a larger system who then becomes a perpetrator? While not an excuse, how does true healing occur? How do we break the cycles and prevent the harmful patterns from repeating?

To me the Witch is the healer in the hut at the end of the village. We are the makers of medicine. To me the Witch is the baker, creating the miracle of bread from the millstone to teach the people how to feed themselves. To me the Witch is the crafter, the blacksmith, creating new wonders, and repairing the old broken things. In Jewish mysticism, it is the holy work of, in its most broad sense, *tikkun olam*, the repair or recreation of the world. To the Kemetic Egyptian practitioner, it is the return to the *zep tepi*, or First Time, through the veneration of the gods. To those in Gnostic Craft, it is the return from exile to the paradise garden. The work is the raising of Atlantis, the return to the Garden of the Gods through the reënchantment of the world. This is my revolution.

While I still certainly get angry, fearful, confused, and depressed, this is not the root of my magic, but is the vision of a new world created by many different actions of restoration. While not as flashy as some, it is a wild and radical concept to actively seek.

So, as a healing practitioner and Witch working with many individuals over the years, I must approach our current society as being sick, rather than being the enemy. While I know conflict is real and there are people acting as my enemy, that cannot be my magical approach. It runs counter to my own vision that all are necessary parts, cells within the body, mind, and soul of the great Goddess herself. It is almost impossible to divorce yourself from every aspect of overculture, so as we all participate, we are all participating in the sickness, and hopefully also participating in the immune response. As a healer, my magical approach is to look to the big picture and act through everyday opportunities to do good, to restore the world through the work that life has brought before me.

In the work of the British occultists influencing modern Witches, particularly Dion Fortune and her experiences in the Magical Battle of Britain, there is the teaching of not just the individual soul and mind, but the folk soul and folk mind of a cultural group, and the national soul and national mind of a country. As an advocate of the three-soul model of a lower self, middle self, and higher self, I would venture the folk, national, and eventual global levels of consciousness possess these three souls as well. Healing comes in the conscious reconnection of each part at one level, and each level with the next.

Each individual participates in their individuality, their familial and ancestral streams of consciousness, the immediate land where they live, as well as the cultural and national levels. We are interacting with the consciousness of the people currently living, the ancestors of the place stretching back into time, the non-human land and faery spirits, and the overarching guiding beings of consciousness and ideals. Unlike Britain or the ancient Pagan world, we do not have, and rightly so, the same concepts of interface between the land, people, and divinity through a sacred sovereignty, so we need to create new magical models. We all need to be simultaneously the sovereigns, healers, and priestesses between the living land and our people.

My magic provides medicine as a spiritual offering to the land, people, and community to catalyze and continue healing. To explore this through your own magical means, I share a working you may employ in your own local area. Choose a place in the land that is appropriate to do the work, an interface point where these things come together. Monuments, statues, memorials, and national parks are all effective points, as well as "vortex" areas and standing stones, and your ritual can be adapted to acknowledge the specific powers to that area.

Prepare a stone, either gathered from the same spot previously, or a stone you feel is appropriate. While a crystal certainly works, it can be a simple rock as a rock attracts less attention and is favorable to a fancy crystal that might be picked up by another. Over the course of a Moon cycle, either new Moon to new Moon, or full Moon to full Moon, work with the stone. Commune with the spirit of the stone, explain your intention, making sure it wishes to aid you in this work. Build the charge of the stone. Bathe it in pure water. Feed it the smoke of sacred resins. Meditate with it. Sleep with it under your pillow, and dream dreams of a new world. Consecrate it. Charge it repeatedly with the intention of healing. Repeat this or something similar:

> *In the name of the Holy Mother and Divine Father, I consecrate this stone for healing, dedicated to the healing of the land, the people, the nation, and the world! May you be a beacon echoing true healing across the land. So mote it be.*

If you want to focus on a specific issue or situation, tailor your invocation to reflect your intention.

Prepare a bottle of sacred water. Obtain one large glass bottle, or several smaller bottles, keeping in mind whether you will need to "sneak" the water into a site disguised simply as drinking water. Using your inner guidance, intuition, divination, or dowsing, determine the appropriate medicines for the water. While you can simply bless the water as you did the stone, as a Witch immersed in the green world, I prefer to add a variety of plant substances, including tinctures, essential oils, homeopathic remedies, and flower essences to the water, creating a blend specific for my intentions. Each form of medicine holds individual healing properties; for the purpose of this magic, any of these forms will help you evoke the plant spirit's aid for this magical medicinal blend. No one should consume this blend personally, rather use it as an offering to the greater land. Use what is at hand. While it is best to make your own remedies when possible, many are available through local handcrafters and commercial preparations. There are many excellent resources on creating your own simple herbal products. While you can add physical herbal matter such as leaves and flowers and seeds, keep in mind that clear water is more discreet when working in a public place.

When dealing with the sickness of the people and the land, I have found these specific plant spirit medicines to be the most helpful:

¶ **Black Eyed Susan** (Flower Essence or Infusion/Tincture of Root) – To face the repressed shadow and bring to light what has been banished to experience healing.

¶ **Blackberry** (Flower Essence, Homeopathic Rubus villosus, or Infusion/Tincture of Leaf) – To face primal fears and prevent being controlled by fears.

¶ **Dandelion** (Flower Essence, Homeopathic Taraxacum, or Infusion/Tincture of Root) – To purify from toxic emotions, specifically anger and tension.

¶ **St. John's Wort** (Flower Essence, Homeopathic Hypericum, Infused Flower Oil, Infusion/Tincture of Flowering Tops) – To protect from evil by bringing in clear light. To banish nightmares. To heal trauma and psychic injury. To reveal fears. To align the soul and ego in harmony.

¶ **Star of Bethlehem** (Flower Essence or Homeopathic Ornithogalum) – To integrate after shock, trauma, accident or abuse. To sooth and reassure after harm.

¶ **Yarrow** (Flower Essence, Homeopathic Millefolium, Essential Oil, or Infusion/Tincture of Flowering Tops) – To provide psychic protection without cutting off empathy and to repair damage done to the aura. Prevents loss of vitality and life force.

¶ **Jasmine** (Flower Essence, Homeopathic Gelsemium, Essential Oil, or Infusion of Flowers) – For anxiety, worry, and stress. To ease depression, fatigue or the feeling of being overburden or overwhelmed.

¶ **Willow** (Flower Essence Homeopathic Salix or Infusion/Tincture of Bark) – To heal grief, bitterness, resentment and grudges, particularly those who feel attached to a victim self-image. Clears illusions and delusions while providing a connection to a strong divine feminine energy.

¶ **Purple Loosestrife** (Flower Essence or Infusion/Tincture of Root) – To manage the experiences of chaos and loss of control in life. To make friends with the wild and unknown.

¶ **Toadflax** (Flower Essence of Homeopathic Linaria) – For promoting tolerance of beliefs and opinions. To encourage listening. To be open to different views, lifestyles and cultures.

¶ **Mullein** (Flower Essence, Homeopathic Verbascum, Essential Oil, Infused Flower Oil, or Infusion/Tincture of Leaf and Flower) – For promoting truth, integrity and conscience. Aids in group harmony and provides a guiding light in times of darkness and difficulty.

¶ **Strawberry** (Flower Essence or Homeopathic Fragaria) – For renewing the enjoyment of life, pleasure and the world. To ease feeling of being drained or that a situation is "killing" you. Hope to go onward.

¶ **Wormwood** (Flower Essence, Homeopathic Absinthium, or Infusion/Tincture of Flowering Tops) – For removal of psychic parasites feeding of vital life force or parasitical people and patterns.

¶ **Datura** (Flower Essence or Homeopathic Stramonium) – For facing the darkness, fear of death or the past, and our own personal "hell." For moving past agitation and opening to clear perception to create our own personal "heaven."

¶ **Belladonna** (Flower Essence or Homeopathic Belladonna) – For cutting the cords to toxic people, places and situation. To look deeply at ourselves and take responsibility for our own toxic action. To experience sensuality and sexuality.

¶ **Monkshood** (Flower Essence or Homeopathic Aconite) – For healing our fears of the future and irrational dreads and phobias. To find the calm center and stillness before taking action.

¶ **Rose** (Flower Essence, Homeopathic Rosa, Essential Oil, or Infusion/Tincture of Petals or Hips) – For magical blessings of the mysteries, healing the heart from old wounds, and building love and trust.

Of course, you may add any medicines from the plant world, as well as any other crystals or bones you feel called to use. Ritually add to the water over the course of the month, and like the stone, bless it, bathe it in sacred smoke, dream and meditate with it, and consecrate it with these or similar words, suited to your specific medicines and intentions:

In the name of the Holy Mother and Divine Father, in the name of the Witch Soul running through me and Witches, from the first to the last, I consecrate this medicine for the true healing of the land, the people, the nation, and the world! So mote it be.

Now using your intuition, guidance, astrology, or divination, choose the appropriate time to place your stone at the chosen sacred site of interface, and pour the medicine water upon the stone. Speak or whisper anything you feel is in accord with your intention, though nothing spoken is needed, and then walk away.

By the first circle of the art
And by black spirits, white spirits, red spirits, gray
I offer this healing medicine to the land and people
By the blessing of the gods, angels, ancestors, and fey
Restore. Renew. Regenerate. Rejoice! Re-Enchant!
So mote it be!

To seal the magic, do the first act of healing and restoration put before you afterwards, often through a stranger. Utter a kind word, perform a supportive action, or simply listen compassionately. Let the magic work.

Nine Garden Allies: Plants for Talismans, Spells & Actions

Raye Schwarz

FOR THE PRACTITIONER who is drawn to plants or has developed a bit more than a basic green thumb, there are many plants which can be grown in urban or suburban settings which offer differing levels of magical assistance, offensive or defensive. Not all of these plants are suitable for ingestion or incense, but all are good candidates for physical amulets, charms, talismans, and rituals.

Crafting protections can happen with advanced intent and planning or sudden needs assembled due to emergency. For either scenario, I keep various items on hand: tiny glass vials, small mesh bags, bits of cloth, joss paper, and empty bullet casings. Many magical plants can be worked with fresh or dried, but think about your intent and which would better suit it. Fresh leaves and roots have more water and lighter vibrations; dried plants often have concentrated oils and energies.

All of the plants below grow in my backyard garden in a naturalized state, meaning they seed and return all on their own each year. Many will grow in a wide range of climates, but check each plant for suitability to your location before planting. For some of these plants, it is beneficial for a human gardener to mind the natural processes of the plants somewhat so that they do not seed and completely take over (i.e., mugwort and poppies), while others will need supplemental watering beyond natural rain so that they better thrive and survive (adjust for your microclimate as necessary).

¶ **BAY LAUREL** (*Laurus nobilis*)/Fire/Sun – Most often seen as a shrub, this plant can also be cultivated as a tree. A symbol of honor and glory dating back to ancient Greece, wreaths of laurel leaves were worn for protection from the anger of sky gods and lightening. To remove harmful energies, the dried leaves can be powdered and burned. Kept whole, the leaves may be hung or put in the corner of your home to ward negativity, or carried to guard against psychic attack. For manifesting magic, spells are sometimes written directly onto the leaves.

¶ **Bittersweet Nightshade** (*Solanum dulcamara*) / Air / Mercury & Saturn – Often used for communicating with the dead, bittersweet nightshade is also collected and hung in bunches near entrances to protect homes and spaces but some sources say it will only work if hidden from view. Other traditions saw shepherd's hang bittersweet nightshade on the necks of their flocks for protection. Bittersweet likes to grow in thickets and hedges, clinging to other plants, and correspondingly is often used for bindings and hexes.

¶ **Lavender** (*Lavandula angustifolia*) / Air / Mercury – One of the most well-known herbs, there are forty-seven different species of lavender. Known for its calming smell and physical healing properties, lavender works well magically for cleansing and clearing. The dried flower buds can be scattered or ground to be burned as incense. Still on the stalks, the flowers can be braided and woven into charms and wands. Lavender offers much support to the magical practitioner in herbal spells and is very good for aiding sleep.

¶ **Larkspur** (*Consolida ajacis*) /Water/Venus – Mythologically, larkspur sprang up from the blood spilled by Ajax when he committed suicide after not being given Achilles' armor. It has been associated with protection and care especially of soldiers and heroes. It was planted near homes and barns to offer protection to both humans and animals. It is described as a specific ward for venous creatures like spiders and scorpions, but is also used in spells and recipes for ethereal threats and ghosts. The flowers can be added to baths, used fresh or dried in herb blends or even scattered to act as a more direct ward.

¶ **Mullein** (*Verbascum thapsus*)/Fire/Saturn – Mullein is primarily known for working with the dead. It can be brewed or smoked for divination work, dream work, to see spirits or to communicate with the deceased. Mullein offers protection from malevolent spirits and also wards nightmares. The dried stalks and leaves have long been used for ritual candles or torches. First Peoples used this plant to return people to their right minds. It is broadly and mistakenly described as a substitute for graveyard dirt, a belief that actually has roots in cultural appropriation and commercialism.

¶ **Mugwort** (*Artemisia vulgaris*)/Earth/Mars & Moon – Mugwort often is used in divinatory or dream work, brewed as tea or burned as incense, but it offers an observational approach, making it good for facing harsh realities. The leaves can be rubbed on magical tools to clear any negative energy that has built up over time and use. The long stalks can be braided or bundled and this herb is sometimes hung to ward malevolent influences near home entrances. It has both Pagan and Christian associations as being worn to ward negative energies along with use as a blessing smoke.

¶ **Poppy** (*Papaver somniferum*)/Water/Moon – Most often, the seeds from the poppy flower are the part of the plant that is used in magic spells. The abundance of seeds produced by the flower pods has led to uses for fertility or good luck, but the soporific effects of the various plant extracts also makes the seeds a favorite for spells that are intended to create confusion, sow legal delays and confound the opposition. Do not allow these to run wild in your yard or on your land, or you will manifest your local authorities.

¶ **Rosemary** (*Rosmarinus officinalis*)/Fire/Sun – Rosemary is another herb very common in magical work, and it is one of the most broad-spectrum protection plants readily available anywhere. Used alone or in blends, rosemary brings cleansing and clearing qualities as well as protection. Sprigs can be hung, and the leaves can be used whole or ground. The scent is said to attract faeries and good energies while simultaneously warding evil spirits and illness.

¶ **Skullcap** (*Scutellaria lateriflora*)/Water/Saturn & Venus – The sedative effects that occur from the physical ingestion of skullcap has led to widespread use in magical spells for calming and restoration, especially after violent situations or attacks. If you participate in protests, you'll want to carry some skullcap. Use specifically to combat disharmony and stress whether it manifests as an internal emotion or an external interaction. Skullcap can also be used for sealing/binding oaths, vows and commitments.

The best advice I ever received about plant work was to start simply and safely, and consider letting the plants guide the lessons. All plant allies have benefic and malefic effects, and either can be employed for defensive or destructive purposes, as the magical practitioner wishes. In this regard, it is often best to use your preferred method of divination or spiritual communication to consult with the plants themselves about how best they feel they can work with you or serve the situation you are addressing.

Age si quid agis.

Bloom where you are planted.

Diana's Protection

Mat Auryn

Oil Recipe:
Three drops Frankincense essential oil

Three drops of Myrrh essential oil

Olive oil

Sea salt

Black pepper

Cayenne pepper

Rue

Angelica

Three thin slices of fresh garlic

A pinch of red brick dust

Three small pieces of broken chain

Three small slivers of lemon peel

Instructions: Begin by lighting a black candle in the name of Diana and a white candle in the name of Lucifer. Recite this passage from *Aradia, Gospel of the Witches*:

I, like thee, was instructed when young by priests to worship an invisible god. But an old woman in whom I had great confidence once said to me, "Why worship a deity whom you cannot see, when there is the Moon in all her splendour visible? Worship her. Invoke Diana, the goddess of the Moon, and she will grant your prayers." This shalt thou do, obeying the Vangelo, the Gospel of the Witches and of Diana, who is Queen of the Fairies and of the Moon. (Ch. XI – The House of Wind)

Add the ingredients to the oil. Then recite the following two passages from *Aradia*, while shaking and mixing your oil:

Then in this dire need she prayed to Diana to set her free; when lo! she found the prison door unfastened, and easily escaped. Then having obtained a pilgrim's dress, she travelled far and wide, teaching and preaching the religion of old times, the religion of Diana, the Queen of the Fairies and of the Moon, the goddess of the poor and the oppressed. (Ch. XI – The House of Wind)

Lucifer was extremely angry; but Diana sang to him a spell, a song of power, and he was silent, the song of the night which soothes to sleep; he could say nothing. So Diana with her wiles of witchcraft so charmed him that he yielded to her love. This was the first fascination, she hummed the song, it was as the buzzing of bees (or a top spinning round), a spinning-wheel spinning life. She spun the lives of all men; all things were spun from the wheel of Diana. Lucifer turned the wheel. (Ch. III – How Diana Made the Stars)

Anoint your hands with the oil and rub your hands around your body as if infusing the oil's energy into your aura. Recite this prayer, and use this prayer when you need protection from all forms of harm:

Holy Father and Holy Mother,
Surround me with protection.
Ward off the ill will of others,
And guard me in each direction.

The New Aradia

Before me Cain brings the Earth's shelter,
Surrounding me in a thicket of thorn.
Protecting me from man and spectre,
And the influences of hate and scorn.

Behind me Lucifer brings Fire's cremation,
Surrounding me with flame and flash.
Burning away any profane pervasion,
Until nothing remains except ash.

To my right Aradia brings Air's dispersion,
Surrounding me in a vortex of swirl.
Blowing away malefic attack's coercion,
To be scattered to the ends of the world.

To my left Diana brings the Water's tides,
Surrounding me in a cooling ebb and flow.
Healing whatever may exist from inside,
All self-inflictions and curses unknown.

The divine around me.
The divine above me.
The divine below me.
The divine within me.

Peace Oil

Jenn Zahrt

CREATE A MAGICAL OIL to bring peace, calm, and protection to any heated situation. This oil harnesses a dynamic talismanic process using the astrology of Mars and Venus to underpin the oil's effectiveness. The herbs alone can do the work, however, adding astrological timing awards the oil with greater potency.

OIL RECIPE:
Olive oil

1 oz. purple loosestrife

1 oz. hyssop

Dash vitamin E oil

Plantary hours of Mars and Venus

New cheesecloth

Double boiler

INSTRUCTIONS: Begin the ritual working on the day of Mars (Tuesday) during a daylight hour of Mars when the planet is in good condition (not retrograde or in Libra, Taurus, or Cancer). Likewise, make sure you can end the working on a night hour of Venus on the day of Venus (Friday), when she is in good condition (not retrograde or in Scorpio, Aries, or Virgo). This will limit your windows of time to make this oil. A bit of advanced planning will go a long way towards a successful working. It also means that you need to plan on tending the fires of your water bath for approximately four days (Tuesday day through Friday evening).

The theory behind this extended duration is that you are taking the heat of Mars and converting it to the coolness of Venus. The work begins with the status quo (the aggressive situation) and ends with the desired outcome (peace, calm, and protection from malevolence directed at you). The water bath should be attended at all times. If you must leave the work, make sure someone can attend to it while you are gone. Once you have found the correct window of time and availability, you are set to begin.

Open your circle according to your tradition and call in your desired allies.

Submerge the herbs completely under a thin layer the olive oil in the upper trough, and ignite the fire on your water bath.

Tend the water bath for the suggested time

Check on the herbs; stir as desired, infusing with peaceful intent.

On Friday, during the night hour of Venus, strain the oil with cheesecloth.

Discard the plant material respectfully.

Close your circle according to your tradition.

Add vitamin E to the finished oil once cool for preservation.

Anoint yourself with this oil any time you must enter a heated situation or face an aggressor. They will be powerless against you, hardly being able to come near you, let alone mount an attack. Placing this oil on shoulder blades, where wings would be, and your solar plexus is very effective in shielding my heart from harm and enables you to wade into hostile waters without injury and pursue my objectives without interference from negative persons.

Dragonroot: A Charm for (In)visibility

Casandra Johns

Smilacena racemosa is a lily native to the Pacific Northwest. It is called "False" Solomon's Seal, but dislikes that name. Solomon's Plume and Dragonroot are names preferred by herbalists and witches of the area because of the way the plant rises and sweeps along the ground, its leaves spreading like wings.

As a medicinal herb, Dragonroot is cooling and demulcent. It works on the respiratory system, digestive tract, and liver. It can be taken as a stand-in for *Polygonatum*, the True Solomon's Seal of the eastern United States, for improving pliability in the connective tissue, indicated by the knuckle-like roots.

This charm works in two ways. It can be used for making oneself less visible to unwanted authority. Interestingly, this charm can also be used with success to bring the right people to oneself while repelling unwanted attention. It is less about invisibility and more about controlled visibility—remaining inconspicuous until the ideal moment.

Find a stand of *Smilacena racemosa* in the early spring or late fall once it has gone to berry. Make appropriate offerings to the land with special attention to local water and air elementals.

Harvest the root of a single plant—this is best done with wooden tools and hands. Notice how the root looks like knucklebones and most roots will have several crowns. Take care to trim and replant the crowns; they will regrow in the next season.

Taking the middle portion of root, separate the knuckles, and clean them well. Place them in a dark place free from moisture to dry. I have found that simply carrying the dried roots is sufficient for this charm, but additional astrological and spell work will add potency. Consider harvesting the root during beneficent phases of the moon and with care for hourly and planetary positions. Consider anointing the dried root with oil and incense according to your practice and the preferences of your personal deities. The chunks of root can be distributed to comrades or placed in oil or fat and steeped, then distributed.

This charm is exceedingly simple, but take care! Use it with clear intention. It has been known to be overly effective at times, preventing drivers from being seen by other cars when thoughtlessly left on the dashboard.

A Prayer to Aradia, in the Wake of Charlottesville

Misha Magdalene

PRAYER IS AN UNCOMFORTABLE SUBJECT for many modern magical practitioners. Most of us were raised in a culturally Christian environment where "prayer" means appealing to deities and spirits many of us do not want to invoke. Within the tradition of witchcraft I practice, though, "prayer" is a broader term which can mean "meditation," "incantation," or "spell" as easily as "appeal" or "plea." Our prayers do call upon gods and spirits to intercede for us, but again, "intercession" is broadly defined.

This is the prayer of my heart, written following the events of 11–12 August 2017, when members of the so-called "alt-right" marched openly in Charlottesville, Virginia in support of fascist, white supremacist ideology, injuring several counter-protesters and murdering activist Heather Heyer.

I offer this prayer to the gods I love, and to my communities, near and far, who live in danger and fear. I offer it to you, if you are so moved, with a caveat: this is no easy prayer. It asks for guidance and protection, but it is also an explicit appeal—a hex, a curse, an imprecatory prayer—against Nazis and other fascists in America. I do not write these words lightly, and if you choose to speak them, neither should you. I do not counsel you for or against this work; I merely offer them for you to read. Do as you will.

Our Lady Diana,
Witch-mother, Witch-queen,
In Your holy name I pray.
I call upon You, Diana,
And upon Your blessed daughter,

The New Aradia

The most holy Aradia,
Saviour of the Witches,
Comforter of the lost and dispossessed,
Teacher of the hidden and secret ways:

The blood of the innocent and the righteous cries out from the earth.
The tears of the wronged burn with sorrow and rage.
The cries of the wounded and bereaved fill the night air.
Our oppressors and murderers walk openly in the streets,
And speak from the highest places in the land.
They posture and preen in their palaces and homes,
And threaten to bring death to us all.

Give us Your favor, Aradia.
Give us Your cunning ways
Guide us through the days which lie ahead.
Mantle us in Your cloak of night
From the eyes of those who would do us harm.
Steady our voices as we speak against evil.
And firm our hands as we raise our fists in defiance.

As for our oppressors,
The would-be lords of power and wealth:
While they glory in hate and feast upon suffering,
I call upon You, Aradia,
To bind their souls and chill their hearts.

Let their weapons fall from their hands, impotent and unused,
Let their limbs quake with the fear of righteousness,
And let them hide their faces from the shame of their own deeds.

Let their families reject them,
Their siblings repudiate them,
And their children shun them and deny their names.

Let their storehouses and coffers be empty,
Their fields be barren,
And their voices be lost on the wind.

While they would work evil,
Let their evil turn in their hands
To strike them down.

But should they turn from evil
And repent their misdeeds,
Then and only then
Let this spell be unwound and dissolve.
Let their injuries cease and their sorrows be lifted.
Let their families reclaim them,
And their voices return.

This, and only this, do I pray of You,
Most holy Aradia,
Most gracious Diana:
By my own hand,
With my own tongue,
And through my own will
Do I pray you grant my petition and prayer.

May it be so.
May it be so.
May it be so.

A Spell To Win a Court Case When Unjustly Detained

Aradia the Rose

Note: To be performed by friends/acquaintances of the unjustly detained. The more friends that participate, the better. Perform anytime between three nights to the night before the court hearing; even better if performed when the moon is in Libra.

ALTAR ITEMS:

Blue candle anointed with rue, vervain and rose oil (or olive oil)

Justice tarot card

Small square of gold cloth

Red string/yarn to tie cloth into a sachet

Small bowl for mixing herbs

3 generous pinches each of dried herbs of Buckhtorn bark, Cascara sagrada, Celendine, Cinquefoil, and 3 Calendula blossoms

Small glass bottle (a 1oz. tincture bottle works great)

Whatever other usual altar items you wish to employ: elementals, deities, athame, etc.

Place anointed candle in center of altar; Justice tarot card above it. Arrange herbs in the north, cloth and string in the east, mixing bowl in the south, glass bottle in the west.

Cast your circle, invoke elementals/quarters, deities (I like the Italic tribal Diana Nemorensis, who provided sanctuary to escaped slaves in her grove, but work with whichever deity feels right to you), and any helpers that present themselves.

Light the blue candle. Take pinches of herbs, and repeat over each one: "Scales of Justice, Hearken and Quaver; Let the judge rule in my friend's favor." Add the herbs to the mixing bowl. Slowly blend the herbs with your fingers, focusing on the light of the candle, and repeating the incantation until your focus begins to blur and a meditative rhythm sets into your body. Stop the chant once you feel that the herbs have been imbued your intent.

Place half the herbs in the center of the gold cloth square, place three drops of the anointing oil on the herbs, and tie it up with the red string/yarn into a sachet. Brew an infusion (tea) with the other half of the herbs by placing the herbs in jar or heat-proof glass measuring cup. Cover with steaming water. Recite the incantation over the brew until the infusion has steeped for eleven minutes (XI = Justice card). Strain the brew and allow to cool on the altar. While the brew cools, continue to chant and meditate on what justice looks like for you in this case, or if performing with a group, create a shared vision upon which to meditate. Once cool, fill the bottle with the infusion, and leave both the bottle and the excess brew on the altar overnight.

Extinguish the candle, devoke, and open the circle. Compost the spent herbs directly into the earth, if possible. Sleep with the Justice card under your pillow until court day. Drift to sleep each night with the incantation lingering in your mind.

On the morning of the court hearing, cleanse your heart and hands with the excess magical brew. Take the bottle of brew and herb sachet with your to the court hearing. At the courthouse, sprinkle droplets of the brew on the ground outside, on the doors of the courtroom, and on the floor of the courtroom. Don't worry, you can do it without anyone noticing. Slip the herb sachet into the detainee's hand when they come into the courtroom, if possible. If not, hold it in your own hand. Continue to recite the incantation "Scales of Justice, Hearken and Quaver; Let the judge rule in my friend's favor" in your mind. Justice will be done.*

Three by Three, So mote it Be

Variation: replace the incantation words "my friend's" with your friend's actual name if you have their permission to do so.

*I have helped multiple friends in the past with variations of this spell. The rulings always resulted in dropped charges.

A Sigil To Protect Protesters & Those Detained by ICE

Laura Tempest Zakroff

Built into this sigil:

¶ prevent arrests of protesters and those who would be detained

¶ provide stamina for protesters

¶ good weather for protesters

¶ that their message be seen, visible, heard, have impact

¶ resilience for detainees

¶ fuel hope

What to do with this sigil: You are welcome to use this sigil however you see fit that is in alignment with the intent of the sigil. It can be worn, shared, drawn in appropriate places, make signs of it, use it for blessings and other forms of protection, and so forth. You don't have to be physically out there protesting to use this sigil—you can use it to lend support to others and bring more focused energy to the situation, guided towards a positive and powerful solution.

A Border Sigil, or a Sigil to Resolve Border Issues & Facilitate Healing

Laura Tempest Zakroff

BUILT INTO THIS SIGIL:

¶ to lend strength to those who need it

¶ promote peace

¶ open (applies to hearts, minds, legal/safe crossing, for those seeking asylum)

¶ recognition of humanity

¶ aid in healing

¶ reunite families

¶ foster community and connection

¶ love

¶ awakening to the issues for informed progress

WHAT TO DO WITH THIS SIGIL: This sigil works well for marking specific places as well as directing the intent to people directly facing border issues. You can share with folks who live or work near borders, or it can be used for safe passage for those crossing country lines, as well as those in danger of being unfairly or illegally retained.

A Witch Bottle for Protection of Home, Family & Community

Kelden

Many things are happening in our society at the moment that have people fearing for their lives and basic human rights. These are dark times, and we all must work hard to defend our lives and the lives of others. While there are numerous ways that we can fight the good fight, the most essential one is to promote the safety of home, family, and community. If we think of our needs as a hierarchy, establishing a baseline of security is necessary before we can work upwards towards other goals. And as Witches, or magical practitioners in whatever form, we have a unique skill set that can be utilized to protect ourselves and others. Of the millions of different spells and rituals that could be worked for these means, my personal favorite is the Witch Bottle.

Witch Bottles are widely known for their use as protective and anti-hexing abilities. Examples of Witch Bottles can be found throughout the history and folklore of Witchcraft. As a protective measure, these are bottles or jars into which one places sharp objects like pins, nails, or broken glass and then fills the rest with their own urine. The magical belief behind these bottles is that they act as decoys. The urine, as an extension of one's self, attracts the harm being sent out. That maliciousness then gets stuck on all of the sharp objects, effectively destroying it. Witch Bottles are classically hidden around the home or buried near the front door.

For our purposes, we will be creating a Witch Bottle focused on trapping any harmful or wanted energy that specifically comes in the form of racism, misogyny, homophobia, transphobia, and all other perpetuations of bigotry. You will need a mason jar, a collection of sharp objects, pieces of mirror (either broken or you can find small reflective disks at most craft stores), googly eyes, protection and banishing herbs of your choosing (I like to use rue, vervain, and rosemary), and a good amount of your urine.

Begin by placing all of the sharp objects into the jar, focusing on the intention of dismantling all harm. Then add in the mirror pieces, envisioning how malicious actions will be reflected back upon their creator. Next, add the googly eyes considering how those actions will be seen by higher power (both legally and spiritually). Sprinkle in your herbs, announcing aloud what each herb stands for (i.e., protection, banishment, justice). Before the final step, have each family member or those who share your residence spit into the jar, contributing their own essences to the decoy. Finally, fill the rest of the jar up with your urine. Give it a good shake and dedicate it to your cause with a few words spoken from the heart.

Either bury the bottle or hide it some place where it will not be disturbed. I recommend replacing the bottle every few months or so, disposing of the bottle as you see fit.

Baityloi: An Ancient Greek Method of Purifying Civic Institutions & Protecting Their Integrity

Gwendolyn Reece

Baityloi are a set of four river stones, consecrated to Apollon Alexikakos, and placed at the corners of civic spaces and sanctuaries to protect them from all evil without and within. This practice originates in ancient Greece, and I have adapted it for contemporary times.

I believe true democracy—the rule of the people—is revolutionary and the struggle for it to be fully manifested is the unending revolution. As a resident of Washington DC, it is my belief that we not only struggle against the perfidy of certain politicians, but that also the unfocused anger about "government" and "politics" creates a toxic astral soup, creating more harm. Additionally, I believe that there are forces, both occult and mundane, that want democracy to fail and that the integrity of the foundations of our democracy is under regular attack. By this I mean things like inhibiting people's ability to vote, gerrymandering, and undermining the separation of powers in order to destroy all checks and balances of those in power. The stones and the shield the *baityloi* create are meant to protect and rarify the atmosphere in the civic buildings where decisions are made that impact us all.

I placed *baityloi* around the Capitol. The reason I believe that they are helping is because of the way in which one of them failed. This working requires feeding and maintenance. I was unable to attend to the *baityloi* for a few months while I was recovering from surgery. When I was able to go back downtown, the stone that was holding the boundary between the Capitol and the Supreme Court had been utterly shattered and the pieces felt extremely toxic. The stone was large enough and in a place that this could not have happened through some random encounter with machinery. It was during this time that McConnell rewrote the rules of the Senate to force the Supreme Court nomination of Neil Gorsuch through. The spell was not powerful enough to stop it, but it was strong enough to be a barrier that had to be destroyed.

This technique works for any civic entity and can also be used for temple protection or adapted for household protection. Here are the steps:

Identify the civic building you want to purify/protect (courts, city halls, capitol buildings, agency buildings, state capitals, governor mansions, the office buildings where politicians actually work, etc.). If you can, assemble a team to help with the feeding.

Go to a local river or stream that is in the same land-base as the area you want to protect. It is best if you already have a relationship with the spirit of the river or stream, but if you don't have one, you need to build one. Before I take stones, I spend a couple hours picking up plastic trash from the waterway and communing. I get all of the plastic trash I can find. If it is a new relationship, you probably want to make a couple of trips for picking up trash before you ask for help. Also, I pick up plastic trash as part of my daily practice as an act of friendship with the waters and to honor Poseidon. This is noticed.

Once you feel like you are in the right place to begin talking about what you need, explain to the river spirit what you are trying to do and why it is important, including why you think the spirit should care. Once you have the water spirit's permission, ask if there are any stones that are willing to serve in this role. Wander around and wait for them to call to you or get your attention. They will need to be large enough and distinctive enough that you don't lose track of them. Traditionally, they were large, white, and round, but I think it is more important that they be of a big enough size that you can find them again, but not so unusual that they call undue attention to themselves. Once you have five, thank the stream and leave.

Clean the stones. Commune with the stones. Take each one and imagine yourself inside of them. Get to know them. Once you know them, introduce them to each other. One of them will be the "control" stone that you will keep at home or in your temple. The addition of the control stone is not traditional, but is an attempt to avoid replicating the failure referenced earlier.

Traditionally, the *baityloi* were consecrated as vehicles for Apollon Alexikakos—the Averter of All Evil. I am a priestess of Apollon and He is willing to do this work. However, if you have a special relationship with another appropriate deity who is willing to do the work, then substitute. Pray to Apollon (or other), and ask Him to be present and to do the work. Explain that you are asking that He claim the *baityloi* as vehicles to purify and protect the integrity of the institution. Take each of the stones and imagine yourself inside the stone and invoke Apollon while you are inside the stone so that His Light is filling it and it becomes a vehicle for Him. Then see the stone inside of Apollon or inside of His Light. Rub Bay oil into the stone and feel it as a vehicle for the Light of Apollon. Once all of the stones are consecrated, it is time to place them.

Prepare a small bottle of olive oil. Dress inconspicuously, and carry the stones in a bag. You are not going *in* any of the buildings, but will be on the grounds. Be discreet. While you aren't doing anything illegal, you also do not want to have to explain yourself. If the olive oil makes you anxious, do not use it. Circumambulate the grounds and look for areas roughly at the four corners around where you feel the edges of the energy. Look for landscape features where the stones will not get picked up by mowers or will inconvenience the landscape artists.

The prayer for this working is, "Apollon Alexikakos, Averter of All Evil, protect (the Capitol, this court, etc.) from all evil, both from without and from within." Use this prayer when you are circumambulating, when you are laying the stones, and later for feeding the stones.

Lay the stones. With each, hold the stone in your hands, once again going into the stone and invoking Apollon Alexikakos in the stone and then see the stone inside His Light. Place it and pour a bit of the olive oil on it. Use the prayer and keep saying it quietly or silently as you walk to the next stone, energetically connecting them. I see the stones anchoring colossus-sized figures of Apollon that hold the corners.

Once the entire circle is laid. Connect them again with the control stone. See the circle become a sphere and see the sphere fill with Light, forcing out any darkness and burning away anything that looks like smog. Put the control stone back in your bag. Go home and place the control stone somewhere where you can give it attention.

At least once a week, connect with the control stone by imagining yourself inside it. Invoke Apollon Alexikakos into the stone and see the light filling the stone, and then see the stone inside of Apollon's Light. See the sphere with the four colossus-sized Apollon figures at the corners. At least once a season, check on the physical stones and feed them energy and connection in the same way you do for the control stone. If you feel comfortable doing so, pour olive oil on them. During the feedings, use the prayer. If you have a team, you can reinforce the physical stones more often. If some get removed, replace them as needed using the same process, but using the control stone for introductions.

A Sigil for the Housing Crisis

Laura Tempest Zakroff

Built into this sigil:

¶ providing home spaces for people

¶ increase affordable housing for all

¶ ensuring the spaces are safe and welcoming

¶ humane treatment, recognition of humanity, reducing the problems that can lead to homelessness

¶ building a better community that supports all of its members

¶ create/promote housing that helps with the flow of traffic, accessible to transit/public transportation

¶ make resources available (physical, emotional, mental needs)

¶ focus on building stability/structure

What to do with this sigil: This sigil is an especially good one to apply to physical locations, but it can also certainly be used to send to specific people or areas. It can be worn, shared, displayed locally, carved on a candle to help focus energy to a related cause, chalked onto walls and spaces, worked into legislation, etc.

Aradia and the Armor of Flames

Devin Hunter

ABOVE ALL THE LESSONS AND PRACTICES, stewardship rises to the top as perhaps Aradia's most defining characteristic. She is the steward of the oppressed and the guardian of those who would fight against that oppression and bestows them with spiritual gifts and protections. Any who would stand up for the oppressed are sacred to Aradia.

As advocates, resisters, protestors, and demonstrators we are often put in precarious situations while in the line of duty. Regardless of how peaceful our intentions may be, the pushback that we receive can be abusive, violent, and at times inhumane. We do not have to be alone or feel alone when this happens; Aradia is there with us, fighting the good fight, even if we do not recognize her. But when we do these things in her name, aligned with her will, we become living representations of her power here on earth. Our ESP heightens, our intuition increases, and our discernment sharpens; giving us the extra juice needed to make it through any situation.

The following working can be done anywhere at any time to instantly align and connect with the spirit of Aradia. The first time I did it was on a train full of protestors as we were on our way to an equality march and rally. Aradia came to me and told me that I was going to be in danger and needed to remain vigilant. She shared this working with me. Though all was well during the day's events, that evening, as my group was headed back to the train station to go home, we were met with violent counter protest. I believe I would have been in real danger had I not performed this working earlier that day. We missed the worst of it just as we were boarding our train and were able to escape the situation without harm. Ever sense, there isn't one march or protest that I go to without performing this working.

Aradia's Armor Working

Take five deep breaths and align your energy body. However you choose to do it, at the end of the five breaths your mind, body, and soul need to be in the same place. Recite the following invocation;

Aradia, protector, mistress of the arts;
be here now before danger starts.
Wrap around me and be my guide,
from our gaze no evil can hide.
Through and before us no evil can pass,
sharp and potent like broken glass.
Flaming armor to protect and defend,
Aradia's might till the very end.

Take a final breath, tilt your head back and then exhale as if snuffing out a candle. As you do this visualize a silver flame sparking from inside and then engulfing you. Repeat as needed or as part of your daily practice to optimal results.

Calming the Inner Storm Spell

Ivo Dominguez Jr.

WHEN WE ARE ENGAGED in the work of struggles, arguments, political actions, witnessing inequity, and such, our thoughts and emotions can raise a great deal of energy. If we are skilled and prepared, we can direct this to more useful purposes. Our thoughts and emotions create thought-forms, durable patterns on the astral plane and within our inner landscapes. The more intense our emotions and focus, the longer they last and the more they manifest in the physical world. If it is more than we can manage, or are already worn down, then this becomes a storm. The patterns of fear and anger swirl around us and cloud our perception. The stinging, pelting rain of energy goads us to make ill-considered choices or embrace despair. Like calls to like, so these energetic patterns stay close to their creator and crowd in upon them. This in turn generates a squealing feedback loop that strengthens the storm, and makes it harder to regain the poise to act with strength and grace.

Here is a spell to calm the inner storm. It is more effective if someone does it for you, but in a pinch you can do it for yourself. It is easier to perform if you are in physical proximity to the person in distress, but if you have experience doing soul travel, astral projection, journeying, or the like, it can be done from a distance. When possible get the person to work with your efforts, if they are too overwrought and agitated, get their consent and let them know you are about to do work for them.

1. USE WHATEVER IS YOUR CUSTOMARY METHOD of opening and preparing to do magical work. Then focus and feel for the person's energy field and for the storm of thoughts and emotions that surround them. Pay attention to all your physical senses, psychic senses, and your intuition and gauge what is present. If the person is open and available to working with you, share your impressions.

2. Close your eyes and envision that you are holding a silver arrow in your hand aimed upwards. Rise on the planes until you are above the storm. Choose to perceive it as a storm rather patterns of emotion and energy. Giving it this shape and name will give you power to disperse it.

3. Now awaken the Four Elements within yourself. Call upon the powers within yourself so you may call upon the powers that exist outside yourself.

Call upon the power of Air, the wind, to push away the clouds, break up the rotation of the storm, to clear the fogs, the precipitation, and so on. When the storm has been dispersed, and you can see the person clearly, surround them with gentle breezes that are cool or warm as needed to bring comfort. If they are cooperating, ask them to breathe in the clear, sweet air.

These storms do not bring down clean water, they are tainted with the sour and unpleasant smells and textures of heavy emotions and thoughts. Aim the silver arrow down and descend. See yourself standing with the person in your inner sight. The silver arrow becomes a sliver pitcher filled with pure water. By the power of Water cleanse whatever stains remain of the storm. See yourself pouring water on their head, hands, and feet. If they are cooperating, ask them to brush away anything that still clings to them.

Now the silver pitcher becomes a silver torch with a flame of red and blue. Walk round the person warming them with the flame. Let the power of the Fire restore their vitality and resolve. Pause in front of them and see their skin glow with lustrous health and vigor. Look deeply into them and see the fire of their great heart. If they are cooperating, ask them to see themselves glowing from within.

The silver torch turns into a silver shield emblazoned with a five-pointed star. Call upon the power of Earth to guard and to shield them. Walk round them with the shield pointed outwards. Then present them with the silver shield and a gesture of acknowledgement. This could be a salute, a bow, a nod of your head, or whatever communicates respect as a physical gesture. If they are cooperating, ask them to see themselves receiving the shield.

4. Close your eyes, both inner and outer, and find your way back to the here and now. Gently disengage from the person's energy if you are still connected. Silently repeat your own name thrice. Do whatever is your customary method for closing down and grounding after doing a working. Check in with the person to see if all is right. If possible, follow up with physical aftercare such as something to drink or eat or a place to sit.

There are many contexts for when this spell may be useful. It works best as a one on one working, but it can be done for a small group simultaneously if you do not have another option. For small group work, rise high enough until you see the storm that is the aggregate of everyone's personal storms. The only major modification is that all the actions are done to the group as a whole. For example, you circle round all rather than one at a time. In the last step, the silver shield becomes a wall of light surrounding the group.

Practice and learn this spell before you need it. Although it can be done cold, reading it straight from this book, the competence that comes from confidence in your abilities is priceless. Use your own words, as many or as few as you like, and your own images. It is the gist and the pattern of the spell that matters, so feel free to modify it so long as the essence of the process holds true. May this spell cleanse, enliven, and protect you in your sacred work.

Two Spells for Water

Annwyn Avalon, The Water Witch

A SPELL TO PROTECT THE WATER PROTECTORS

Acquire a two-sided shell, such as a clam, oyster, or cockle shell. Then acquire a photo or write down the names of the water protectors you want to protect via spell work. Place their taglock in the shell with a quartz point and a piece of black tourmaline; you can also add a few sharp objects such as shark teeth, hawthorn, or rose thorns or shell fragments. Bind the shells together with a black string and charge it with your intent. Place it on your altar and pray over it or imbue it with magical energies every full moon.

TO BIND COMPANIES WHO HARM THE WATER

To bind companies that harm our oceans you will need to acquire something that has their logo on it. You can print out one from the internet if you like. Take this logo and place it in a clam or oyster shell that you found on the beach. Next use either bindweed, pieces of a fishing net you have found on the beach, or tangled fishing line. It is best to use objects you find on the beach or by the river. This helps to clean the area and put trash and debris to use. Wrap the shell with this tangled mess. If you used all organic material such as bindweed, take it to where three rivers meet and bury it near where they intersect. If you have used recycled trash such as netting or fishing wire, bury it in the western corner of your yard or a friend's yard. Do this on a waning or dark Moon. Call upon the local water spirits to aid you and leave appropriate energetic or organic offerings.

Water Devotional & an Oath to Protect the Water

Lisa Bland

WATER IS LIFE, FOR ALL. It is the great sustainer of our physical bodies, through which we can do our magic and work in the world. This devotional includes an optional vow to protect the water, should you feel called to do work in your area for water protection with organizations or community groups.

This devotional is a call to honour the water that surrounds us, that is within us and others, and a call to protection. It is meant to take place outside, near your largest body of accessible water.

Gather some water from your property (whether from your tap, a pond, a stream, or other sources). Take some that you can drink as well if you are not using tap water.

Center and ground yourself, and prepare any sacred space as your tradition indicates.

Think about the water before you, and in your area. Connect to the water spirits of the place and ask about it's health. Following your connection, say aloud:

> *I honour the water of this planet,* (pour some water)
> *I honour the water of these lakes, streams, rivers, and oceans,* (pour some water)
> *I honour the gods who are the water.* (pour some of the water out, singing to the water gods if you work specifically with them)

Reflect on the drinking water you have brought, and how nourishing it can be for you. Reflect on the safe water you have access to, and the communities of all our brothers and sisters, especially our Black and Native brothers and sisters, who may not have clean water.

Reflect on the gift of clean water. Fill the water with light energy as you drink it in, and nourish yourself.

As you pour out the remainder into the water flowing near you, say aloud:

I honour that water that nourishes my whole being.
I honour the water that nourishes all beings.
May all beings be protected from illness.
May all beings receive clean water.
I give blessings and love to the water.
I give blessings and love to the water protectors.
So mote it be.

(optional water protection vow)

I call upon the water protectors' spirit.
I call upon the water spirits, warrior gods and goddesses of water.
I pledge my energy to water protection.
I vow to make magic manifest in protection of the water.
May the elders and ancestors guide me in this work.
So mote it be.

Take whatever time you need to and finish up your work according to your spiritual practice (energy raising, closing a circle, etc).

Creating a Sun

Annalun

More a yoga exercise than a spell, "Creating a Sun" is encouraging—creating power, integrity and happiness within. It makes one able to spread positive energy and light in the world.

You can do this sitting or standing. Make sure your arms and hands are free to move. Visualize your connection as a witch between the earth and the heavens above. Visualize that you are the perfect mixture of both, that with your inhale, you breathe in the earthly energy of our Great Mother, and with your exhale, you share your breath with our Lord the Sun king.

When your breath is stabilized, put your arms and hands in front of your sacral chakra in shape of a circle. Visualize drawing up this earthly energy through your body while you inhale and stretch your arms up in front of your body and reach above your head.

When your hands reach your forehead, turn them from facing upwards to facing downwards and continue with the movement of stretching your arms up towards the sky. Visualize your fingers cuddling with sunbeams, drawing down some of their energy towards yourself and the earth. While exhaling, slowly pull your arms down around your body creating a giant circle—creating an orb of sunlight around yourself.

Repeat as many times as you need to fill your body with divine light.

I sometimes end this by saying a quote from the *Emerald Tablet*: "As above so below, blessed be!" In Swedish, we say:

> *"Jag står med en hand i jorden, en hand vid solen, bägge har mig fast!"*
>
> "I stand with one hand within the earth, the other reaching the sun, (they're) both holding me steady."

Prayer to the Great Mother

Jay Logan

Holy Mother, in whom we live, move, and have our being.
From you all things come, and unto you all things return.
You, who are of many goddesses and gods,
Who are of many spirits and lifeforms,
And yet remains one shining blue orb racing through the heavens:
To you I sing many praises and adorations;
To you I give my love everlasting, kissing your rich earth
and green grasses;
To you I pray on behalf of my species.
Help us Great Mother.
Help us to save ourselves.
Help us to topple those in power;
Those who ignore our prophets Cassandra,
Our scientists and researchers who warn of the dangers our climate
will bring if we do not change;
Those who lead our people in shortsightedness and greed;
Those who would wring the last drop of your black blood
from the earth
And sacrifice the future of our world in the process.
Join your will to ours, Great Mother.
Open our hearts and our minds and our eyes to each other.
Grant us the strength to join our wills together in solidarity.
Hand to hand—Heart to heart—Spirit to spirit.
Grant us the strength to change our fate;
To change the web of our wyrd, the weaving of our web;
To preserve the working of our ancestors,
the heritage of our people

So that we may continue to tell the stories of our gods,
    the legends of our heroes,
So that we may continue to dance, sing love, and make
    beautiful art and magic.
To you I pray, Holy Mother,
In whom we live, move, and have our being.
From you all things come, and unto you all things return.

Blessèd be.

Composed in 2015.

Blood Moon Eclipse Ritual

Irina Xara[1]

Note: This was originally written during a blood moon eclipse that took place very late-night/early morning. Please feel free to alter any of this to fit a timeframe to be done near total or maximum lunar eclipse at any particular time of day. This ritual may be enacted solo or with a group.

Clear/set your space appropriately.
Up until this point in the eclipse, you may chant, meditate, pray or rest.
Go into a meditative state of mind, or do this upon emerging from sleep.

We remember those executed under the name "witch."

We remember all victims of sexual crimes and intimidation who have never spoken their perpetrators' names or identities.

We remember all nameless victims, especially the transient, poor, transpeople/Womxn of Color, sex workers and femmes from other high-risk groups.

We remember the named victims. [Name victims you wish to remember here.]

We pray/ask for restoration, peace and resolution for their families, partners and social circles.

---

[1] In acknowledging my own identity as a cisgendered white woman, I must acknowledge that I have related blind spots when working towards inclusive language and concepts in a ritual. It is my hope that this text will be interpreted as a guideline and jumping-off point rather than an edict on How to Do Things. Please feel free to alter language and gendered designations as you feel, and know that these words are only a loose container for energy that is shared. You are valid and valued.

We make the earth fertile with [her/hir/their/_____] ashes.

Her/hir/their children/students/chosen/family go forth to teach compassion, care, justice, mindfulness, and conscious action.

We do all we can to restore our taxed earth.

We amplify our/indigenous voices who are intertwined with our lands. [If you are indigenous, please feel free to alter this line to reflect your work better, or to name your nation(s) if you wish.]

We honor cycles, replicable data, healing, both indigenous and otherwise, and science as tools for right relationship with our planet.

We hold space for the restoration of men and manhood, free from the toxic traditions of masculine construction. We uphold bravery, sensitivity, and kindness for all gender expressions.

Those of us who bleed or who are initiated into uterine mysteries honor our body's shedding with the blood moon, and we create space for fellow womxn and femmes who do not resonate in this way or who may no longer bleed.

We honor the grief of all traumatized by the medical industry, especially the transphobia, birth rape, disregard for consent and disregard for communication therein.

We honor the Womxn of Color and global womxn victimized by medical trials and brutal, nonconsensual experimentation.

We honor all those denied access to reproductive and sexual agency, autonomy and healthcare.

We honor and remember all children who have been victimized.

We honor the ancestors and their wisdom, especially our womxn, femme, and gender-nonconforming forebears, and those who fought for sexual, gender and racial/intersectional justice. We hold a space of deep gratitude for all their work.

We honor all those who experience obstacles against their showing up for justice, including employment status, class/financial reasons, race/ethnicity, disability status, incarceration status, and family obligation.

We do our active work to understand our more-privileged intersections and how we may have been complicit in misogyny, white supremacy/racism/prejudice, colonizing attitudes, externalized or internalized, and other forms of entitlement, unconsciousness, disrespect, and oppression. We hold space for those we love of all genders and backgrounds doing this work, without doing the work for them and while exercising appropriate boundaries and self-care.

We bless our land, our human and animal circles, our families both blood and chosen, our partners/spouses, our students and teachers, our co-creators, our extended communities, and the unities of our experiences as human beings.

We love. Fiercely, bravely, relentlessly, tenderly, and in spite of. We heal. We fight and nurture, in just balance.

We are present, with honor for life in body, and for our bodies. Spirit seeks wholeness with body. We listen to our bodies.

Close the energy.

Optional sample affirmations appropriate for eclipse work that can be added before or after ritual:

I practice silence actively.
I respond rather than reacting.
I have everything that I need.
I grieve as I need to, unaccountable to anybody's discomfort with my grief.
I voluntarily, consciously release attachments to what no longer serves me.
I act appropriately as I can and in consideration of other peoples' agency.
I am grounded.

Or write your own!

Resistance & Resilience / Resilience & Resistance

Irisanya Moon

THE WORLD HAS BROKEN MY HEART, more times than I can admit or know or count. The lies. The lies upon lies. The fake news. The silence. The tweets.

It wasn't that long ago that I could see the fires move along the mountains of Santa Rosa. It wasn't long ago that the things I used to say were "somewhere else" are now showing up on my front door. And there are days when believing in myself or in others is challenging, if not impossible. My heart forever wants to believe that people are inherently good and reasonable. But my heart has been broken.

"...the broken heart can cover more territory."
—Adrienne Maree Brown, "Spell for Grief or Letting Go"

Scanning the territory of my life, the broken times, the down times were the ones where I was collecting the tools I needed. I didn't know it at the time, of course. I didn't believe there was another side. I was knee deep, sometimes waist-deep, in doubt.

And it is hard to move from that place.

If there is one thing that Aradia has stirred for me is that we can be in the muck, in the deep, in the places of WTF and still resist. We can call upon the stars, the Moon, our friends, our wildest, fiercest hope to bring us back to the moment when we are needed. We can use the tools we have and know that we are a part of a "we."

We are needed. We need to be here today and tomorrow.

Without our strength and the tools to repair what breaks in our own bodies, we are not the best resistance. We are too tired. We are too dazed. We are too stuck.

Cultivating resilience can look like:

¶ **Slowing** – Take a breath. Don't answer the phone or that important text for 33 seconds. Find ways to stop the allure of right now. Slow down. Whatever needs you will still be there after you catch your breath.

¶ **Separating** – Walk away from the places that are too much. Step back because if you don't, you could run away. Disengage for an hour, a day, or more. Whatever it takes to find the breath again, to know your heart as steady and grounded.

¶ **Cleansing** – From cleansing with the smoke of burning things to salt baths to loud screams and long tears, let it go. Get rid of the things that stick too easily. Remove the words, the worries, and the whys until you are lighter. Burn them. Rinse them. Let them go. Every day. Every night. Good spiritual hygiene is important.

¶ **Protecting** – Talismans, incenses of myrrh and frankincense (and other resins), and a circle cast. Mirrors. Wards. Shields. Salt at the door. A witch's bottle. A chant that reminds me I am not alone. I call to the gods, and I listen to the ones who answer.

All of this is a foundation for resistance,
And a spell of resilience,
And a spell for resistance,
And a foundation for resilience,

Today and tomorrow.

A Sigil To Prevent Burnout, or the Anti-Burnout Sigil

Laura Tempest Zakroff

Built into this sigil:

- abundance (in terms of what energy and resources needed)
- maintain a sense of balance as needed
- amplify good health
- a pilot light that inspires, cleanses, and invigorates
- protection
- allow for rooting, grounding (of ideas, of mind and body)
- a focus on other, the umbrella, community

What to do with this sigil: This sigil can easily be used personally to fight burn-out as well as aiding a larger community. You can wear it, drawn it on yourself, paint it in healing colors, place it on your altar or put it in a place where folks need to be renewed and refreshed. This would be a good sigil to "consume"—via food or beverage.

A Spell to Reclaim Your Sovereignty

Deborah Castellano

ITEMS NEEDED:

Myrrh

Charcoal, lit

Fire safe container

Fresh flowers (either picked or bought)

Floral wire

Floral tape

String lights or electric candles

Two bowls

Rose quartz crystals

Handful of dried lavender

Chalice

Sacred liquid to drink

Salt water

A candle, offerings

Tarot deck

Potential sovereigns: Your own goddesses (which include ancestors and spirits), a historic queen you admire, St. Elizabeth of Portugal, Mary Queen of Heaven, Diana, etc.

Arrange your electric candles or string lights into a circle big enough for you to do your work. Pour salt water into one bowl. Arrange the lavender and rose quartz into the other bowl. Arrange your small shrine to your goddess(es) along with the candle and offering. Ask for her/their blessing to guide your hand during this work. Use words that are meaningful to you. Pour sacred liquid into chalice. Put the myrrh on the charcoal. Anoint yourself with the smoke. Wash your hands, your third eye and the top of your head in the salt water. Then, say:

> *I am sovereign over my own body. My body is sacred. I am sovereign over my own spirit. My spirit is sacred. I am sovereign over my own mind. My mind is sacred. I am sovereign over my own heart. My heart is sacred. I am Sovereign. I am sacred.*

Start making your floral crown. If you do not already have a lifetime of experience making them for May Days, Beltanes and festivals, use the internet to either watch a video on how to do so or get step-by-step instructions, whichever is easier for you. Consider making a practice crown pre-rite. While making your crown, sing songs that are meaningful to your sovereignty, trancing or meditating on your sovereign status.

Rest your crown over the bowl of rose quartz and lavender. Put your hands on your crown. Repeat:

> *I am sovereign over my own body. My body is sacred. I am sovereign over my own spirit. My spirit is sacred. I am sovereign over my own mind. My mind is sacred. I am sovereign over my own heart. My heart is sacred. I am Sovereign. I am sacred.*

Touch the crown to your navel, your heart, your throat and your forehead. Put the crown on your own head. Repeat:

> *I am sovereign over my own body. My body is sacred. I am sovereign over my own spirit. My spirit is sacred. I am sovereign over my own mind. My mind is sacred. I am sovereign over my own heart. My heart is sacred. I am Sovereign. I am sacred.*

Hold the chalice in your hands. Focus on what you want to bring to yourself. *As a sacred Sovereign, I won't want for...* (love, strength, compassion, abundance, and so forth)

Drink what is in the chalice. Thank your goddesses for their presence. Draw a Tarot card. That is your omen for your work. Reflect. Hang your crown over your bed and put the bowl of rose quartz and lavender next to or under your bed.

House Cleansing Wash

Lyssa Heartsong

THIS RECIPE IS PERFECT as a general floor/house cleaning watch to clear out stagnant and accumulated energy or purify a ritual space or temple. You can modify the ingredients with additional herbs or substitute out the lavender if you have allergies, etc., but this is the general base I use. It is great for quarterly cleanings, washing altar items, cleaning the portals in your house (windows, mirrors, etc.), and cleaning spaces that you are just moving into or vacating. Feel free to use it more frequently as an all-purpose cleaning wash. If your house is a center for political action, social justice work, or helping those in need, this can be a good regular wash in times of trouble to keep the space clear and add to the general protection of a space.

INGREDIENTS:

1 large pot of water on the stove, or, one 1–5 gallon of hot wash water in a bucket

1 pinch of salt for purifying

½-1 cup white vinegar/gallon of water

1 lemon, cut in half

A few hefty splashes of Florida water

1 large handful of lavender or other herbs of your choice in a muslin bag or teaball

Optional: A splash of your favorite general cleaning soap or ammonia at the end if you have a particular grimy job. (And don't ever mix ammonia with bleach, folks. Please read your labels!)

PROCESS: Many of these ingredients have multiple uses in different traditions, so you have some room to modify them to your purposes. Charge each item as you add it to the water. My words vary from working to working, but I have included a few examples in the process, but really, this is a simple wash, and you don't need to overthink it. The exact order isn't important, save for the salt, which comes first.

Get the water hot on your stove or as hot as your tap will allow and fill the bucket.

Purify the water with salt.

Cut the lemon in half. *Cut through that which binds us, protect this hearth from harm.* Add it to the water.

Add the lavender and/or other herbs, charging the water with your intention at each addition. (Cleansing, purification, etc.) *Bless this space with calm and clarity.*

Add the vinegar. *Cleanse this space from harm and illness, old despair and ill intentions, and all that would harm those within.*

Add the Florida Water. *Bless this space and all within with health, safety, and protection.*

Hold your hands over the water and visualize additional energy pouring into it. By my will, so mote it be!

Now go and clean your space as needed!

A Spell for Good Housekeeping

Stephen Pocock

At the Aradia-based California Witchcamp in the summer of 2018, I was working in trance with descendants. This was imparted to me. It has been described as "good housekeeping" by my friend and mentor, Urania.

Salt by the front door
Twigs by the back door
Pebbles under the bed
Water on the hearth
Leave a window open
And a flame going

Some notes:
The hearth could be your stove. We have a fireplace.
A flame: of course a candle should not stay lit when you are not home. It has been suggested that a stove or water heater's pilot light will suffice.

I wrote a spell to go with this that can be used to strengthen if needs be:

With salt and twig,
Pebble, water, and flame
Protect this hearth and home
From sorrow, harm, and pain

A Ritual for Remembering Our Power & Remembering What We Are

Amanda Bell

CAST YOUR CIRCLE, CREATE YOUR SACRED SPACE. Stand at the altar of your choosing. Speak these words in that sacred space, so the wind will carry them. Bring a mirror if you've forgotten what you are and speak to yourself.

Go ahead and burn me. The fire will change me,
 transform me to ash.
The rains will carry me into the earth, where I will nourish the seeds,
 and help them grow.
When they grow, my magic will be carried from bud to bud on the
 winds and by the bees.
They will carry me to my familiars.
My magic will mingle with every living thing on this planet.
Burn me and I shall be everywhere.
The air you breathe, the water you drink, the earth that nourishes
 you, and the fires that keep you warm.
These will all bear my mark.
And, World…you will bear my mark.

I fear not the Fire, that transforms me.
I worry not over Water, that carries my heart.
I envy not the Earth, that holds root my soul.
I argue not the Air, that shares my truth.
It is not for these elements to cause fear, for they are our gifts.
With them, and our intent, we are creators of magic.
Blessed Be our Freedom

We gather by moon light, we gather by sun.
We assemble in groves, or a solitary one.
We care for the crossroads, we protect the keys.
We share these rites, may we ever be free.
We stir the cauldron, we tend the seed.
We claim our freedom, so mote it be.
So Mote It Be.
So Mote It Be.

Composed in April 2012

A Sigil to Build and Strengthen Community

Laura Tempest Zakroff

Built into this sigil:

- enable a healthy flow of communication (speak/listen/acknowledge/understand)
- emphasis mutual respect
- help build a stable foundation and common ground
- inspire dynamic/positive leadership
- instill integrity
- be inclusive, incorporating diversity
- encourage participation/gathering

What to do with this sigil: This sigil is ideal for being placed in community spaces: on the walls, drawn on floors, made into altar cloths or arrangements of flowers, placed on banners, assembled at the base of a bonfire before it's lit. It can be used to bless festivals, rituals, Pagan Pride events, and other gatherings.

An Invocation for Freedom

Patti Wigington

Hail, you gods and goddesses of liberty and justice!
Watch over those who fight for freedom,
and keep us in your hands and hearts,
protecting us as we rise and resist,
as majestic as mountains, as mighty as endless waves of grain,
against the swelling tide of hate and tyranny.

Hail, you gods and goddesses of liberty and justice!
Hold us fast and resolute, shoulder-to-shoulder and unwavering,
as the dark tower of oppression begins to crumble and fall.
Grant strength to the disenfranchised and the forgotten,
the frail and the marginalized,
the poor, the tired, the huddled masses yearning to breathe free,
and to all whose voices lift up on their behalf
in the names of those unheard.

Hail, you gods and goddesses of liberty and justice!
Grant independence to people around the world,
no matter what their faith,
and give us the words to speak out against those
who would grind us beneath their boot heels,
who wish us to stay silent,
who tell us to ride in the back of the bus,
who insist the words of the new colossus are only for a chosen few,
who refuse to see that dissent is the foundation of history.

Hail, you gods and goddesses of liberty and justice!
Guard us, so that those far from home may return to their families,

the scales of justice will balance again,
that liberty shall again be an inalienable and self-evident truth,
and those harmed by hate will once more feel safe.

Hail, you gods and goddesses of liberty and justice!
Hear our call, and light up the sky with the red rockets' fire,
the torches of strength shining, sovereign,
that we may find our way back to you,
and bring together this land of the free, this home of the brave,
once more, in unity.

Acknowledgments

STRAIGHT TO THE POINT: Jenn Zahrt is nothing short of amazing. Late one night while I played reluctant host to Insomnia, the idea for this anthology made itself known. Already beyond busy with an overloaded schedule, I thought, well, that would be a wonderful thing, but no way, not right now, not possible in the time-frame needed. Besides, I know how long it takes to get things published through the usual means. Yet the idea was more persistent than a hungry cat, so on a whim I approached Jenn with the concept. Despite her also equally busy schedule, she was totally on board.

Then came the tricky part of putting a call out for submissions with a very small window. Yet, we received quite a huge stack from folks all over in such a short time. I have so much gratitude and appreciation for every single person who was inspired to share with us their work. Thank you to everyone who submitted, whether selected or not. Your interest in this project alone helps to give it life and light the way for change. Also much thanks to our reader team who helped us go through all of the submissions. Together, we have manifested this book.

I would like to thank Robert Mathiesen for his inspiring research into the history of Leland's *Aradia*, and especially his esoteric guidance way back in my college years—and now. Last, but not least, much love for my partner Nathaniel and his relentless support of my work in all of its forms.

Contributors

ANNALUN is an artist and teacher of fine art. Her speciality is based on a communication between herbs and plants in her surroundings where naturalspirits and her own experiences of shamanic meditation take form in rather big paintings. She is born from a long tradition of Scandinavian folk magicians and has been practicing folk magic and witchcraft since childhood. High Priestess of Gardnerian Witchcraft in Sweden.

ARADIA THE ROSE has practiced eclectic Witchcraft since 1994. Half Greek, half Welsh-Scottish-Chickasaw, she was taught how to use traditional plants for food, medicine, and protection from curses. In 2003, she invoked Aradia and journeyed to Italy. She heard a voice on the wind while at the Temple of Diana at Lake Nemi. Shrouded in mystery, the message has left her ever searching for its meaning. Today, you can find her foraging food and medicine www.theevillageapothecary.com, hunting, and a home birth midwife. Aradia the Rose is the creator of Aradia's Festival of Torches (www.aradiasfestivaloftorches.com), a 4–day festival that honors freedom from oppression.

MAT AURYN is a Witch, professional psychic, and occult teacher through- out the New England. He is currently a High Priest in the Sacred Fires Tradition of Witchcraft and an initiate in Black Rose Witchcraft. Mat has had the honor and privilege of studying under Christopher Penczak, Laurie Cabot, Devin Hunter, Storm Faerywolf, Chas Bogan, Jason Miller, and other prominent Witchcraft teachers and elders. He runs the blog *For Puck's Sake* on Patheos Pagan. He has been featured in various magazines, radio shows, podcasts, websites, anthologies and other periodicals. His first book *Psychic Witch* is due in Autumn of 2019. Learn more about him at www.MatAuryn.com

ANNWYN AVALON is an initiated Priestess and Witch whose path focuses on water and serving the spirits and gods/ess that dwell within. Her focus is on Sacred Wells, Rivers and Lakes but she enjoys time at the sea shore as well. She expresses her path through Witchcraft, watercolor painting and sacred movement which focuses on devotional and theatrical water themed belly dance pieces. She is the founder and High Priestess of Triskele Rose Witchcraft, the nine-month Water Magic Course and is also the authorof the book *Water Witchcraft: Water Magic from Celtic Countries* (Weiser, 2019).

H. Byron Ballard, BA, MFA, is a western NC native, Witch, folklorist and writer. She is senior priestess and co-founder of Mother Grove Goddess Temple and the Coalition of Earth Religions/CERES, both in Asheville, NC. Her books on Appalachian folk magic include *Staubs and Ditchwater* and *Asfidity and Mad-Stones. Embracing Willendorf: A Witch's Way of Loving Your Body to Health and Fitness* launched in May, 2017. Her latest book *Earth Works: Ceremonies in Tower Time* explores cultural collapse. Byron is currently at work on *The Ragged Wound: Salving the Soul of Appalachia.*

Amanda Bell has identified as a Witch since 2009. Before that, she self-identified as a humanist, who just so happened to read tarot cards, worship the moon, speak to trees, and discuss the inner workings of religion and faith with anyone that stood still long enough. Consciously working with Aradia since 2011, Amanda has shared all that she has learned with anyone seeking to find their way and discover their own path. She is currently the founding member of Indie Deck Review and the owner of Salt and Shadow Tarot.

Lisa Bland is a Witch with a holistic healing focus in professional life, community service, and her private Witchcraft practice. Lisa is an advocate for marginalized groups, with a passion for prison ministry and hospice care for Pagans, for mothers and children as a breastfeeding educator. She is an advocate for inclusive Witchcraft with a calling for water protection with local aboriginal communities. Lisa has been an active volunteer with local community and national groups in political advocacy groups, health care, and pagan organizations, and internationally with the Temple of Witchcraft and Covenant of Hekate.

Deborah Castellano's book *Glamour Magic: The Witchcraft Revolution to Get What You Want* is available for purchase at your favorite bookstore. She writes about Glamour Magic at *Charmed, I'm Sure* (www. charmedfinishing-school.com). Her craft shop, The Mermaid & The Crow (www.mermaidan-dcrow.com), specializes in old-world style workshop features tempting small batch ritual oils and hand-spun hand-dyed yarn in luxe fibers and more! She resides in New Jersey with her husband, Jow and their cat, Max II. She has a terrible reality television habit she can't shake and likes St. Germain liquor, record players and typewriters.

Ivo Domínguez, Jr. has been active in Wicca and the Pagan community since 1978. He is an Elder of the Assembly of the Sacred Wheel, a Wiccan syncretic tradition, and is one of its founders. He is a part of the core group that started and manages the New Alexandrian Library. Ivo is the author of Keys To Perception, Practical Astrology for Witches and Pagans, Casting Sacred Space, Spirit Speak, Beneath the Skins, and numerous shorter works. www.ivodominguezjr.com

Storm Faerywolf is a professional author, teacher, poet, and practicing warlock. He has been initiated into various streams of Witchcraft, most notably the Faery tradition, where he holds the Black Wand of a Master. He is the founder of his own lineage, BlueRose, with students and initiates in eight countries. Author of *Betwixt & Between* and *Forbidden Mysteries of Faery Witchcraft*, he is committed to re-forging the ancient connections between humankind and the Hidden Kingdom. He makes his home in the San Francisco Bay area and travels internationally teaching the magical arts. For more, visit faerywolf.com

Lyssa Heartsong (Kelly Grejda) is an artist and writer living in Oakland, CA after having lived most of her life on the East Coast. Lyssa embraced eclectic witchcraft early in her youth thanks to voracious reading habits and gaming. She has studied with T. Thorn Coyle and is a member of Morningstar Mystery School, in addition to currently studying the Anderson Feri tradition with Anaar Nino. She spends most her time dyeing fiber, spinning yarn, sketching, and painting. She has previously been published in *The Star of Opening, a Morningstar Mystery School Anthology*. The fruits of her fairytale superpowers can be found at www.etsy.com/heartsonghlamourie

Devin Hunter (San Francisco Bay Area) is a bestselling author who holds initiations in multiple spiritual, occult, and esoteric traditions and is the founder of his own tradition, Sacred Fires and co-founder of its offshoot community, Black Rose Witchcraft. His podcast, The Modern Witch, has helped thousands of people from all over the world empower themselves and discover their psychic and magical abilities. Devin is the co-owner of The Mystic Dream, a metaphysical store in Walnut Creek, CA, where he offers professional services as a medium and occultist.

CASANDRA JOHNS is an antiauthoritarian herbalist and animist living in Salem, Oregon with her partner and daughter. She studied clinical herbalism and plant/human relations at The School of Traditional Western Herbalist and The School of Forest Medicine. Casandra spends her time running the press at House of Hands, studying graphic design, illustrating botanical and anatomical minutia, and working with Gods & Radicals as a copy editor and occasional designer.

PHOENIX LEFAE is equal parts blue-eyed wanderer and passionate devotee of the Goddess. She attended her first Reclaiming ritual in 1995 and she's been hooked ever since. An initiate in Reclaiming, the Avalon Druid Order, and Gardnerian Wicca, Phoenix has had the pleasure of teaching and leading ritual across the United States and Australia. She is a professional tarot reader, rootworker, writer, shop owner, and Priestess. Find out more about her at Milk & Honey (www.Milk-and-Honey.com).

JAY LOGAN is a long-time resident of the Pacific Northwest in the would-be sovereign state of Cascadia. He is an initiated priest of Chalice Hart, a local Wiccan coven, as well as a mystes of the Naos Antinoou, a queer polytheist community devoted to Antinous, which he serves as priest and Mystagogue. A librarian by trade, he enjoys reading, providing information and resources to the public, knitting, and dancing under moonlight at the Witches' Sabbat.

MISHA MAGDALENE is a multi-classed, multi-geek, multi-queer Feri Witch with a gender studies degree and an odd sense of humor. They write the *Outside the Charmed Circle* blog for the Patheos Pagan channel, and are currently writing their first book for Llewellyn Worldwide. They live on occupied Duwamish territory in the Pacific Northwest with their polymath partner, their precocious daughter, and far too much coffee-making apparatus.

Residing in Northern Minnesota, KELDEN is a practicing Traditional Witch over nearly thirteen years. His Craft is highly influenced by the history and folklore of Witchcraft as well as the natural landscape where he lives. In addition to following his path as a Witch, Kelden holds degrees in Human Services, Psychology, and Marriage and Family Therapy. When he is not working his job as a therapist, Kelden enjoys reading, writing, playing ukulele, being out in nature, and working in his garden. You can read more of Kelden's work on Traditional Witchcraft on his blog, *By Athame and Stang*, www.patheos.com/blogs/byathameandstang

IRISANYA MOON is a Reclaiming Witch and initiate, teacher, writer, priestess, ritualist, and Feri student. She has taught classes and Witchcamps in the US, Canada, Australia, and the UK. She is a blogger for Patheos, Moon Books, and Pagan Bloggers, and has been published in *Witches & Pagans* and numerous anthologies (*Every Day Magick, Seven Ages of the Goddess, The Goddess in America, Naming the Goddess*, etc.), as well as a contributor to the upcoming book, *Elements of Magic*. She is writing a book to be released by Moon Books in 2019. www.irisanya.com

CHRISTOPHER PENCZAK is a modern Witch working in the Temple of Witchcraft tradition and community he helped co-found. His practice focuses on the intersection of Love, Will, and Wisdom as an ethos for today's Witch, and focuses upon relationships with the plant realm, the patterns of astrology, and the use of trance in the Craft. He is the author of many books, including the *Temple of Witchcraft* series and *The Mighty Dead*. His vision is of an evolving Witchcraft culture making magic accessible to all, yet preserving the heart of the mystery. For more information, visit www.christopherpenczak.com and www.templeofwitchcraft.org

STEPHEN POCOCK is an Oakland-based Witch in the Reclaiming tradition. He is devoted to Hecate in her many aspects. Stephen works with fire and smoke as a meat alchemist. In ritual, Stephen puts his theatre training to use for invocations. At home, he pores over magical and other texts and listens to a wide range of music. Stephen lives with his wife Jill, his teenage twins, a cat and a snake. The learning never stops. We are Aradia.

GWENDOLYN REECE is a Witch, Philhellene, Theosophist, and Neoplatonist, serving Apollon and Athena within the nation's capitol as a priestess of the Theophania Temple, including serving Apollon as mantis. She found a place for herself in contemporary Paganism in the mid-1980s. She is a priestess of the Assembly of the Sacred Wheel, President of the Sacred Space Foundation and graduate of the Gryphons Grove School of Shamanism. She lectured extensively for the Theosophical Society for sixteen years and continues to guest lecture. Gwendolyn is faculty at American University and she uses her academic position to conduct research on contemporary Paganism.

RAYE SCHWARZ is a polytheist alchemist, currently residing in the Pacific Northwest region of the US. They spent more than a decade co-collaboratively creating alchemical ritual and fire-tending at events including FireDance (CA), MayFire (NV), Wisteria (OH), and Illumination (OR), and have studied laboratory work with Robert Allen Bartlett. Raye has presented at Mysterium, GeekGirlCon, ManyGodsWest, PantheaCon and the Magickal Women Conference. For the last six years, they have been focused on growing and alchemically working with saffron, and are working on crafting the Paracelsian medicine known as The Elixir of Propriety.

AIDAN WACHTER is a talismanic jeweler, dirt sorcerer, and the author of *Six Ways: Approaches and Entries for Practical Magic*. A magical practitioner since his teens, Wachter found Aradia in the early 1990s on the shelves of Curios & Candles in San Francisco. Always fond of the more anarchic streams of philosophy, it spoke to him in a way much of the neo-pagan Witchcraft of the time did not. He lives in the mountains of New Mexico, where the night skies are clear as black glass and allow for the easy counting of star-mice year round.

PATTI WIGINGTON is an author and educator in the Pagan community. A licensed minister in the state of Ohio, she is the founder and High Priestess of Clan of the Stone Circle, a Celtic Pagan tradition. With thirty years of practicing Witchcraft behind her, Patti has been the host of About/ThoughtCo's Paganism & Wicca website since 2007. She is the author of two books on modern Witchcraft, *Wicca Practical Magic* and *Daily Spell Book for the Good Witch*. She has a degree in History from Ohio University, and facilitates workshops around the Midwest when she's not busy with magical mayhem.

Irina Xara is a writer, proofreader, social media manager, professional intuitive reader/healer and performing artist from the Los Angeles area. Her writing foci are Middle Eastern dance, feminisms, social justice and spirituality. Her spiritual practice is a solitary one that blends Abrahamic traditions, neopaganism, Kabbalistic and other mystical influences and folk magic.

Jenn Zahrt PhD is an author, publisher, astrologer, alchemist, and teacher of cultural astronomy and astrology. She researches the many forms of astrology emergent across human cultures past and present, with a special focus on early twentieth century German culture. She is the founder of Revelore Press and the creative director of the Sophia Centre Press. She co-edits the *Verdant Gnosis* series on esoteric herbalism with Catamara Rosarium and Marcus R. McCoy. She teaches and lectures domestically and internationally, and she sort of lives in Seattle, wa. Discover more of her work at: www.jennzahrt.com

Laura Tempest Zakroff is a professional artist, author, dancer, and designer. She has been a practicing Modern Traditional Witch for over two decades and is also a member of nectw (New England Covens of Traditionalist Witches). Laura holds a bfa from the Rhode Island School of Design, and trained at Fleisher Art Memorial in Philadelphia and the South Carolina Governor's School for the Arts. Her work has received awards and honors worldwide, and has been published in numerous books and magazines.

Laura's art embodies myth and the esoteric through her drawings and paintings, designs, and dance movement. She is a member of The Mechanist & The Star Goddess—a music and dance ritual experience, and the main creative force behind #WeAreAradia.

Laura is the author of *Sigil Witchery*, *The Witch's Cauldron*, *The Witch's Altar* (with Jason Mankey), and *Weave The Liminal: Living Modern Traditional Witchcraft*. She blogs for Patheos as *A Modern Traditional Witch*, Witches & Pagans as *Fine Art Witchery*, and contributes to *The Witches' Almanac, Ltd.* More at www.lauratempestzakroff.com

Resources

SINCE IT WAS PUBLISHED IN 1899, *Aradia or the Gospel of the Witches* by Charles Godfrey Leland is in the public domain.You can visit www.sacred-texts.com or find versions online. There are also numerous updated versions with additional commentary and information. Recommended editions to check out in print by the following publishers: Phoenix Publishing Expanded edition (1999); The Witches' Almanac (2010); Troy Books (2018).

Other recommended books:

Earth Works: Ceremonies in Tower Time
by H. Byron Ballard, Smith Bridge Press, 2018

Keys to Perception: A Practical Guide to Psychic Development
by Ivo Dominguez Jr., Weiser Books, 2017

Forbidden Mysteries of Faery Witchcraft
by Storm Faerywolf, Llewellyn, 2018

Magic for the Resistance: Rituals and Spells for Change
by Michael M Hughes, Llewellyn, 2018

The Witch's Book of Power by Devin Hunter, Llewellyn, 2016

The Temple of Shamanic Witchcraft: Shadows, Spirits and the Healing Journey by Christopher Penczak, Llewellyn, 2005

Six Ways: Approaches & Entries for Practical Magic
by Aidan Wachter, Red Temple Press, 2018

Sigil Witchery: A Witch's Guide to Crafting Magick Symbols
by Laura Tempest Zakroff, Llewellyn, 2019

CPSIA information can be obtained
at www.ICGtesting.com
Printed in the USA
BVHW07s2004011018
528974BV00002B/38/P